Part Two of

REQUIEM

a trilogy

KILLING TIME

a play by Francis Warner

The strength of sin is the law.

I Corinthians 15:56.

OXFORD THEATRE TEXTS 3

First published in 1976 by
Oxford Theatre Texts

represented by Carcanet Press Ltd
266 Councillor Lane
Cheadle Hulme
Cheadle, Cheshire

Photographs and cover design
by Billett Potter of Oxford

Throughout the REQUIEM where photographs
differ from text, the text should be followed

SBN 85635 198 9 – cloth
SBN 85635 199 7 – paper

*Printed in England
by W & J Mackay Limited, Chatham*

All enquiries regarding performing rights should be addressed to:
P L Representation Ltd., 33 Sloane Street, London, S.W.1.

KILLING TIME was first performed by the Samuel Beckett
Theatre Appeal Company at the Jordanburn Theatre, in the
Royal Edinburgh Hospital, on Friday, August 22nd 1975 as a
part of the Edinburgh Festival Fringe. It was designed and directed
by the author.

The cast was as follows:

Chalone	*Peter Rutherford*
Squaloid	*Gerald Tarrant*
Phagocyte	*William Sleigh*
Kuru	*Evie Garratt*
Quark	*Andee Cromarty*

In this production the part of anonymous fighter in Act One
Scene Four normally doubled with the part of Kuru was played
by *Karen Wadey.*

For the REQUIEM and its MAQUETTES: Company
Manager Tim Prentki. Stage Managers Gully Stanford, Patrick
Nelder, Colin Thompson, Tim Prentki. Production Managers
Tex Greenwood, Kenneth Bonfield. Lighting Designs, David
Colmer, John Leventhall. Chief Technician Richard Wall.
Wardrobe Rona Treglown, Gill Oswald, Jenny Hughes. Pro-
duction Adviser Adriana Lawrence. Posters Laura Potter with
Henry Moore, Elisabeth Frink.

Characters

Chalone   *a man of about sixty-five*

Squaloid   *a man in his late forties*

Phagocyte   *a man of about thirty*

Kuru   *an attractive woman in her late thirties*

Quark   *a girl in her late teens*

There are two Acts

Act One

The stage is a giant human brain.

Kettledrums. Downstage right a bell set up ready for tolling. Enter CHALONE (*pronounced Kay-loan*) *stripped to his waist, hooded as an executioner, a revolver stuck in his belt, in his left hand a pair of scales.*

He stares at audience through slits in his hood, then tolls bell slowly and regularly, as for a passing bell. Then

PROLOGUE

CHALONE   The crematorium of war is here. Death creeps in our homes, our streets, our kitchens, disfigures the children in their beds. Even the animals have fled. There are no birds in the sky. The proud oaf man is pinned by his arrow of time, and our eggshell peace blown like thistledown in a whirlwind, (*Throws away scales*) the olive burned up like petrol. In the theatre of war a soldier must take life as it comes. On the battlefield there are no philosophers; only the raw wound of the mind. (*Draws revolver*) Jackal days teach survival. Humanity? If humanity is a race then the game is lost, the future has run out. Greatest power is now in the hands of childish men, and when savagery is enthroned, justice must be an executioner, a jailor of free air, arbiter of both ends of the spectrum. Between the ultra-violet and the infra-red we reap the harvest of tears.

He tolls bell again. Then

Perhaps there is a greatness in man only brought out in war. What a frail hope. We are more like severed worms, caravans of weasels. When two dogs fight and one of them can grip no longer, he rolls over and offers his throat, and the other turns away. It's a natural instinct that prevents all dogs fighting to the death. Even wolves have a code for killing their kind. But man and the fox are deformed. (*Takes off his hood to reveal his face*) The fox kills far beyond his need for food, for pleasure, until exhausted. And the human baby is anonymous until his teeth grow. Then the shape of the jaw gives the parents' likeness. He can bite. There is no innocence save lack of experience; and man, being a questing creature, cannot accept life on those terms, so war is a fever in our brain. Struggling for wisdom we throw away that which we'll soon long to have back. Carnage returns to Europe. A huge evil is unleashed. Once more the terror and the flame. As I look into the crimson sunset, I fear for the coming darkness. The fact that life must end makes it valuable, precious. Violence is tomorrow. Come!

Exit. Kettledrums.

SCENE ONE

Dark. Two male voices simultaneously.

Who goes there?

Lights up on stage to reveal sandbag trench, V-shaped, apex upstage centre. SQUALOID *stage right faces* PHAGOCYTE *stage left. Each has rifle at the ready, bayonet fixed, challenging the other. Their uniform, battledress, should be unidentifiable, neither specifically German nor British. A dead soldier (a dummy) with bullet through head, lies downstage right throughout scene.*

SQUALOID   Look, don't kill me and I won't kill you. Right?

PHAGOCYTE   I'll risk it.

SQUALOID   How do I know it isn't a trick, and you'll shoot me after all?

PHAGOCYTE   Look, mate. It was your idea. I don't want to kill.

SQUALOID   Right! I'm an old hand at this. Because I spoke cynically, that doesn't make me a cynic, does it?

PHAGOCYTE   Share any bread? Something to drink? Whisky? Local wine?

SQUALOID   Cheese. You know, I can't wait to look back on these good old days.

PHAGOCYTE   Nor I. What's going to happen?

SQUALOID   Who knows? The city may fall. If I were to tell you we are waiting to be overrun, you'd panic. Don't just do something. Sit there. Fag? Here you are. (*They light up*)

PHAGOCYTE   Thanks. What shall I call you?

SQUALOID   Squaloid. And you?

PHAGOCYTE   I'm Phagocyte.

SQUALOID   Bully! Now, if we all did this no one would be hurt, would they?

PHAGOCYTE   Have you killed many men?

SQUALOID   Me? Ha! It's my third war. Great War, Second War, and now this. Your first man, it's like catching your first pike. Death makes a man of you. What's the news down the line?

PHAGOCYTE   Desperate, but not serious. Bloody cold night.

SQUALOID   Well it's dawn now. You want to watch out for the steam from your mouth on a winter morning. I could see it.

PHAGOCYTE   Look at that sun! The splendid late crisp full sun of a winter dawn. Back home now I suppose the bare leaves are almost off the trees.

SQUALOID   How can they know what it's like when winter cracks the bones in these trenches. The cold's like the wind on the top of Snowdon.

PHAGOCYTE   Trees bare, fields frosted, brown furrows. Ah!

Spring, if only you knew how welcome you are after a bitter winter.

SQUALOID   You're soft. What kind of a soldier are you? You don't want to kill and you think about home. You'll soon be cracking up! But I get sentimental at times, bored to tears or buggered with fear. God I can't wait till the Drill Halls are filled with Saturday dancers, women fumbled outside in dark car-parks, the baker whistles once more on his rounds, the Friday fishmonger hoots his horn in the village lane. Want a banana?

PHAGOCYTE   No, thanks. I took a bet on once and ate fourteen in twenty minutes and made myself sick, so now I don't eat them.

SQUALOID   Look, mate, you can't be fussy here. I've been a runner. I've had many a can of hot soup off a dead man.

PHAGOCYTE   What do you mean?

SQUALOID   When I was young.

PHAGOCYTE   I've been burning bread to make a binding agent for diarrhoea. Lice, too. I don't know anything more humiliating than my first discovery of lice. I was so upset I burned my trousers to get rid of them. Then for a long time I had no trousers.

SQUALOID   We crack and eat them. In those days provisions were good. Very good. We were in trenches then, not foxholes like these. They served us well. It's amazing the number of different ways you can cook bully-beef. Make the tea in the billy-can you've boiled your bully-beef in, grease floating all over your drink. Ah! it was good.

PHAGOCYTE   I can't stop myself shaking when I'm not expecting it.

SQUALOID   It's not war you should fear. It's fear. Every man's a brute underneath. (*Searches pockets of dead soldier, then sits on him and listens*)

PHAGOCYTE   I was in Egypt. A staff sergeant in Cairo, as I had a
              little Arabic. I'd only picked it up in the army so it
              wasn't very good. I was asked to come to the Special
              Branch officer to help him. He swore me in and
              said any orders under seal I had to do. I'd never
              done any active service at that stage. I had to
              watch a girl of twenty-seven who was called Solange
              to report on what she did. I shadowed her for about
              a week; went out with her, came to know her quite
              well. One does in these circumstances. Then one
              day I was called in to sign for a sealed envelope. It
              was wax-sealed inside, and said – in hand-writing –
              Solange was in the building. On no account was she
              to leave the building. 'In your hands.' Then the
              signature.

SQUALOID   Go on. (*Rises and goes over to* PHAGOCYTE)

PHAGOCYTE   I asked her into a room upstairs. 'Come in!' I said.
              'I've something to say to you. Let's throw some
              light on this by opening a window.' They were
              French windows. (*Pause*) She had an unfortunate
              accident. (*Pushes* SQUALOID) I pushed her.

SQUALOID   What's an atrocity between friends?

PHAGOCYTE   It was reported in the *Egyptian Mail* as suicide, and
              they put it down to boy-trouble. You see all sorts of
              people walking about in the street wounded, with an
              arm or a leg missing, but there are thousands more
              whose wounds don't show. In here. (*Pointing to his
              own head*)

SQUALOID   These things have to be done. If I were to remember
              what I'd done in war I wouldn't lie straight in my
              peace-time bed. You can't afford a conscience.

PHAGOCYTE   A month later a civilian came up to me in a bar and
              said, 'Thank you for doing what you did.' 'Why?' I
              asked. 'It's not your business to know,' he said, 'but
              it may interest you to hear that it was because of her
              information that a Red Cross ship was torpedoed.
              Good-bye.' A visit on leave last week looking down
              over a cliff brought it all back.

SQUALOID   You're a knee-trembler. I know what you mean. It's funny. I was sent to tell a tank of ours to turn a bit to the left and deal with a machine-gun post. I knew the officer was going to pick on me as a runner so I volunteered before he could, and ran out there and waved my arms about. 'What are you doing, Tommy?' he said in the tank. 'I've been sent to ask you to deal with that machine gun that's firing at you. It's firing at me, too.' 'Alright, Tommy! Not worth your jumping up; just get behind the tank while I swing round.' I nipped behind and got spattered with mud from the caterpillars, right in my face. He just ran over that machine-gun post and squashed six Jerries. It was only a shellhole. They hadn't a chance. Funny. If it was now I couldn't stomach it, yet then – I don't know if it's youthful exuberance or something – I didn't even think about it. Just glad to be able to get back to the line.

PHAGOCYTE   Your eyes are sunken.

SQUALOID   Lack of sleep. Oh, I'd sooner be in the assembly trench waiting to go over the top than a runner. Those Very lights are hell. Light as day. Five miles of duckboards over drowning mud with Jerry potting at you as you cake-walk. I was first down on my face. No hero me. I was so small it saved my life. They kept missing me. But the hours waiting to go over the top were the worst.

PHAGOCYTE   And yet if you fly above a city and look down and ask if that is freedom, the answer must be 'No.'

SQUALOID   Fly? Huh! We had mules.

PHAGOCYTE   Mules?

SQUALOID   Oh, far better than horses. They'd pull the transport out of a ditch as no horse could. They were fine if you didn't let them turn their heads, but if they once looked round they'd be galloping back to base like nobody's business. You couldn't hold them. The worst was when one of the transport mules ran loose into no-man's land, Jerry at night shooting at it one way, Tommy the other, till one gave it a bull's-eye. One ran about for hours with three legs. It was the Passchendaele salient. Shaped like a carrot, I can't think of any other way to describe it. Jerry each side of us narrowing us in, and us stuck up there in the point.

PHAGOCYTE What was the worst?

SQUALOID When the C.O. said, 'A raid's required. We need a prisoner.' That was to see what state the Jerries were in. Oh, many young officers were killed like that. Dark trench, only a bandage round your arm to tell whether you were friend or foe, everyone killing everyone. They had to sneak over and come back with a prisoner, and most got snuffed themselves. Terrible. Then coming back there were your own jittery sentries. Just the same with a runner. When a sentry said 'Friend or foe?' we got bollocked if we said 'Friend'. 'Name & Regiment! Name & Regiment!' The best fighters were the Northumberland miners. Used to fight among themselves if they'd nothing else to do. Like the Irish. Go into a pub, the Irish will, have a few drinks, then step outside and take off their coats, have a ding-dong, and then go back in to finish their drinks. Funny sort.

PHAGOCYTE Christ, there's a mortar! They're coming closer! Do you think we can get out of this alive if the city falls? Oh! Another!

SQUALOID That's nothing. We were in a dug-out once, but a Jerry one. The door facing the wrong way. The C.O. said, 'Come here a minute.' I stepped over to him and two seconds later, WHAM, a minnie-werfer hit all the other five of us straight through the open door. You couldn't bury that. Just shovel it to one side and leave it for the rats. Oh, if you slept on the top level, just underneath the ground, that's where the rat's 'ud run. You'd wake up and find rat-shit all over you. One bit my nose when I was asleep. It swelled up like a cherry.

PHAGOCYTE   Did you take many prisoners?

SQUALOID   Aussies! There were thirteen Jerry prisoners . . . One for each of us. We were taking them back through the lines. Some real rough Aussies came up and said 'Where are you taking them?' 'Back to base,' I said. 'Oh no you're not,' they said and shot them all. They were unarmed! I couldn't have done that. When I got back the Colonel said 'Where are the prisoners?' 'Some Aussies came and shot them, Sir.' 'Oh well, saves taking them any further,' he said and forgot all about it.

PHAGOCYTE   Good God!

SQUALOID   The front-line troops were more aware of the value of life, I suppose. They had more compassion for their opposite numbers on the other side. In many cases the front line were older men. It was the support troops behind, the young and unblooded, or the ill or 'medically inferior' who were the devils. Many a prisoner taken in the front line and passed back didn't survive the support troops.

PHAGOCYTE   I see. (*Pause*) Was your wife waiting when it was over?

SQUALOID   I wasn't married, though I'd a girl. When I was in the trenches she used to send me intimate letters and nude photographs of herself. When I was back, I found I much preferred the photographs to the nude woman. She had pains and smells and moods and talked too much. Give me an absent love, and something to look forward to! Oh, but do you mean did they worry if their wives had been unfaithful? We were bloody glad to be home, and didn't take much notice of that sort of thing. (*Pause*) I survived the war, came through all that bloody war and then, if I was in a minute after 9.30 in the evening, my Mother would weigh into me. (*Laughs*) She'd still tuck me up in bed at night. (*Suddenly alert*) Who goes there?

Blackout as both shoot into wings offstage right simultaneously.

SCENE TWO

CHALONE, *pompous and fussy, wearing half-cut glasses, full-bottomed wig and codpiece, black gown open down the front. He lectures the audience holding a pointer with which he gestures to the large photographs of the brain he has before him. Recommended photographs: DeArmond, Fusco and Dewey, 'Structure of the Human Brain, A Photographic Atlas', Oxford University Press 1974. Page five, lateral surface as photograph i; page nine, medial surface as ii; cover photograph as iii; page three, superior surface as iv.*

CHALONE   (*Pointing to photograph i*) There's something wrong with this. Nature went astray. This is the cerebellum, at the back of the skull behind the brain stem, and under the great hemispheres of the cerebrum. Cerebellum means 'little brain'. If the cerebellum (*Pointing to photograph ii*) is split down the middle, the folds form a pattern which resembles a tree. This has been called from time immemorial the tree of life. (*Pointing to photograph iii*) Unfortunately, it is also the tree of death.

We know the wiring circuits of the eyes, the olfactory organs, and the sexual. More generally, the reticular formation of the brain on the main brain stem keeps you aroused (*Pointing to a member of the audience*) and awake! We know the senses of arousal. We know the seven nerves of the cortex. First, climbing fibres for comedy; second, mossy fibres for tragedy. As tragedy is the higher mode, the mossy fibres stimulate the largest number of cells and provoke negative feedback. Comedy on the other hand reasserts balance and peace, so the climbing fibres spring naturally from the two inferior olives of the brain stem. Third, fourth, fifth and sixth, the indigenous ones, each with their own characteristics, and running to and fro among each other – basket, granule, Golgi, and stellate. And finally, an overall judge, with checks and balances, serving as sole master of the system, (*with modest pride*) Purkinje.

Chalone is the stopping agent that prevents the brain growing too large for its skull, as bone grows at a different rate. (*Pointing to photograph iv*) The two parts of man's brain process material in parallel, the laughter and the sadness, and the overlapping of their fields creates orientation, enables the brain to discern differences of intensity, and so make judgements. The left hemisphere reacts to visual input with verbal response, and the right hemisphere to tactual responses. The left hemisphere, for example, cannot draw a square. No.

It would be a miracle were it not for one basic fact. The only moral direction of the entire unit is towards survival. This it has, of course, in common with animals. What distinguishes man from animals is not speech, writing and such, for which there are many analogues, but his ability to commit suicide. Even lemmings don't do this intentionally. They swim madly, hoping to get to the other side. (*Pause*) But you can argue that this ability of man also implies its opposite, and that – may – save us from the holocaust. On the answer to this question hangs the future of the world. Goodnight. (*Exit*)

SCENE THREE

*Right of stage centre a table in shape of human brain, over which hangs a woman (*KURU*) nude save for large silver wedding bell from neck to just above waist. This covers the harness by which she is suspended; the impression, however, must be of a recent suicide by hanging. As clapper in wedding-bell she swings slowly to and fro, face upstage unseen.*

At stage left end of table sits QUARK, *as a very young girl, in baby-doll nightdress and briefs. Behind her, centre-stage right, is her barbed-wire playpen, raised as for a birdcage, built like a concentration-camp guard-tower, into which she climbs at end of scene. At other end of table sits* CHALONE *facing her, in full-bottomed wig etc. as for previous scene, reading a child's comic. At appropriate moment* QUARK *passes the marmalade to* CHALONE *by placing it on the feet of* KURU *and then gently, absentmindedly, swinging it across to* CHALONE. *Neither takes any notice of* KURU *until the very end of the scene when* CHALONE *catches sight of her at the last moment.* QUARK *remains unaware of her.*

CHALONE   Eat up, girl. It's nearly time for school. (QUARK *splutters with her mouth full*) Now, Quark, wait till your mouth is empty. Think of others.

QUARK   I'm sorry, Chalone. It's a holiday. May I leave the table?

CHALONE   If you must. (*Reads his comic*)

Exit Quark stage left.

CHALONE   (*After a pause he looks up*) Stop running under the mulberry tree after blackbirds when the leaves are falling!

Re-enter Quark.

QUARK   Don't be a dead hand on my growing up. Teacher's had a puppy and she's not married. (*Anguish*) Will she have to leave?

CHALONE   Rules are there for a purpose. For the sake of others. The restrictions – are you listening? The restrictions hammer home the lesson that restraint, and conformity to so-called 'natural' order, are too repressive for man to bear. He claims he needs to indulge all his human inclinations. Initial liberty and hedonism give way to the disillusionment and cynicism of a society where self-interest is aligned with motivation. We don't want that, do we?

QUARK   Why are you so strict?

CHALONE   The judge is condemned when the guilty are acquitted.

QUARK   You won't let me take gifts from boys.

CHALONE   A gift destroys the heart. I want to have a serious talk with you, Quark. Remember; the state bureaucrat knows better than the individual expert. Now, society depends on the integration of those functions that prostitution siphons off. We've a vested interest in keeping home sex as a reward for a good husband.

QUARK   (*To audience*) Though he is peevish, yet he is my father.

CHALONE   Talking to yourself, child? (*Pause*) Are you charmed, Quark? You seem impervious to the fact there's another person present. Honour your parents!

QUARK   Does marriage bring both of you pleasure?

CHALONE   Pleasure has nothing to do with happiness, Quark, as you'll learn. Look at this nutritious but hideous food! Pass the marmalade, will you?

QUARK *places marmalade pot on* KURU'*s feet and swings it across.*

QUARK   Oh, I know it went wrong, but you said if you take a saucepan that's caught, and dunk it hot as it is in cold water, you can rescue the food, provided you don't scrape the pan. I don't know why it works, but it does. (*Radiant*) It's magic!

CHALONE   It's burnt. The trouble with you is you cling to a love of the game of life, and as your Mother will tell you it's no game on the game. Now, up to your playpen if you've no school, and practise strangling your dolls.

QUARK *climbs into playpen and strangles one doll violently and, as* CHALONE *leaves, hangs, with glee, another.*

CHALONE   (*Reading*) 'The pleasure lies in the fourth longest kiss.' Very true, very true! (*As though calling upstairs*) Are you coming down to breakfast, angel? I'm leaving. See you tomorrow. (*At last moment catches sight of* KURU) Oh do stop trying to attract attention. (*Exit*)

SCENE FOUR

Semi-dark stage. Enter anonymous figure (KURU) *dressed in full leathers, including head and hands, open knife in* *hand, alert and prepared for sudden attack. Prowls stage. Sudden entry of second figure (*PHAGOCYTE*) also dressed in full leathers, knife in hand. They stalk each other, fight, and finally in a clinch* PHAGOCYTE *stabs anonymous figure in back. He unzips victim's tunic and reveals and exposes pair of woman's breasts where both he and the audience had expected a man's torso. He drags stabbed woman off.*

SCENE FIVE

Music: anthem 'O Lord, look down from heaven' by J. Battishill sung as centrestage is revealed a large brain out of which is hollowed a confessional box, penitent stage left, priest stage right. The priest is CHALONE, *who sits. He performs the conjuring trick 'the multiplying billiard balls', until there are three. Then one by one they disappear.*

Scream off-stage right. Then PHAGOCYTE *enters from stage left to confess.*

PHAGOCYTE   (*Distraught*) Father, I've done a terrible wrong.

CHALONE   (*Gently sanctimonious*) Weakness is only the reverse side of human potential, my son.

PHAGOCYTE   I stabbed a woman, thinking it was a man!

CHALONE   Women are life's music. Music is life's light, and love of children its radiance.

PHAGOCYTE   I feel I've severed a life-force.

CHALONE   True damnation is to have no wish to be saved. Even in the choicest spirits the gold must be passed through fire to purge it of dross, and man's spirit must be stabbed broad awake. In the crucible of religious tenderness, wisdom is not a property of the dead but of living experience.

PHAGOCYTE   Curses return. They do! We took a good-looking girl, used her for a few days, then killed her because we were bored and satiated, and she complained and coughed too much.

CHALONE   Confessions do take a good deal out of one. Pray that our delight in the richness of joy make us not blind to the wickedness of evil.

PHAGOCYTE   I woke in the night with tears down my face.

CHALONE   You have mated unchecked? Tears cost too much, yet are inexpensive, even so. Avoid the shallowness of those people who see the supernatural merely as an extension of their own sexual instincts. Turn humiliation into potential dignity. Beware the third person singular, and the third person plural: he, she, them. Love can only use the first person plural: we, us. Then all our best endeavours no longer turn awry.

PHAGOCYTE   I didn't mean to stab her!

CHALONE   If intentions were the criterion of excellence, every sermon would be a masterpiece. A man's true humility is the inverted image of his real nobility.

PHAGOCYTE   You see to the centre of things, and see clearly.

CHALONE   The peace of this world is no more than the peace in each one of us; in you, in me: the love that refuses to hate. It's the withdrawal of imagination we must study; in marriage, in torture, or a mercenary. Perhaps we must each take the nightmare journey from Gethsemane to Golgotha, the way of the gallows, guillotine, and gas-chamber. All the proud men. Wonderful and horrible things are soon to be committed in this land. Who understands the deep mystery of personality? Oh Lord, how long? I go the way of all the earth. Who am I to forgive?

Exit stage right.

PHAGOCYTE   Hullo? (*Looks out*) He's been swallowed by the day. I feel cleansed.

PHAGOCYTE *comes out and goes in to the priest's compartment.*

Enter QUARK *in white, as for confirmation.*

PHAGOCYTE   Be seated, child. What must you confess? Is it sexual?

QUARK   I've the mistral in my eyes!

PHAGOCYTE   Tell me all.

QUARK   I've only just learned. I was one of twins. One twin, my brother, had been dead two months in the womb. I was the bigger one, and the doctor says that as I needed room I kicked it right to the back and in the process either broke its umbilical cord or strangled it with it. I can't bear to call it *him*. Born a murderer! Oh God forgive me!

PHAGOCYTE   Merely a matrix rejecting its product. Do you play chess in the mirror?

QUARK   Oh, I will, I will. Anything to make up for it. Do you think God will forgive me? I can only see the future in distortion, like a sundial in water.

             SQUALOID *appears from stage left with finger on lips, and changes places with her. She leaves, perplexed.*

PHAGOCYTE   Delight is eternal while tragedy passes. The mystery of sex was dispelled in a monastery garden when our bishop Gregor Mendel crossed a garden pea with green seeds with one with yellow seeds, and the seeds of all the daughter plants were yellow. So it is with humans. The seven chromosomes of his pea match the seven nerves of our cortex. We are the pawns of night manoeuvres. Be reassured, my dear, as the light is dark. Some genes are dominant, and some recessive. I will simply place my hand on your lap, and give you peace. (*Screams*) A Man!

SQUALOID   (*Seizing Phagocyte's wrist*) Right! Caught you. Come along for a little explanation. Come out into the coat-racks.

             Exeunt. Fade as Tractus 'Absolve Domine' from Roland de Lassus Requiem for Five Voices begins.

SCENE SIX

Enter KURU, *dressed as a little girl, pushing a bath chair in which sits* QUARK *dressed as a very old lady. As the scene progresses they gradually exchange ages and change places.* QUARK *carries an ear-trumpet.*

KURU   How are you feeling, Grandmama, on your cardboard wedding?

QUARK   (*As an extremely peremptory old lady, opening her vast fob-watch and looking at it*) Is the universe open, or is it closed? Poussette, dance round a little more, would you? A little more pushing.

KURU   Summer and play are very much in the air.

QUARK   It's one of those mornings when the world is a new creation. I feel young again.

KURU   It is I who'll soon be in the catacombs.

QUARK   If you go about thinking of yourself as old, you'll be old. There are two speeds of days, fast when happy. You grow old quicker so happiness is extremely dangerous, it ages you. It is only now I am ripe I can enjoy it.

KURU   You must almost be a part of history.

QUARK   When history is forgotten, so is gratitude. You end up like an Englishman in America, outclassing the classless.

KURU   How's your ear-trumpet, Grandmama?

QUARK   Like a daffodil. Now, Poussette. You must understand the traumatic shock of a very rich person forced by sudden circumstance to earn, with dignity, the bare essentials of life.

KURU   Wouldn't you rather the comfort of an Old People's Home?

QUARK   Give my back to the smiters? The backbiters? Kiss cheeks with those that pull me by the hair? Are you dumb? (*Pause*) I'm so glad we stayed that night in the male brothel. It was like being lodged in a garden of cucumbers.

KURU   Grandmama, I feel I must remind you, my name is not Poussette but Kuru.

QUARK   We are a binary system. Paired Hollywood stars that revolve around each other: one seen, the other unseen. What was your name?

KURU   Kuru.

QUARK   This is like my old seafaring days. There's the port! (*Pause*) But it's not the right one! Now, let me see. Kuru. That's an unusual name, dear. Isn't it a spreading disease caused by eating live brains?

KURU   It's you are U.K. backwards. Very British.

QUARK   Impaired mental and motor functions, presenile dementia, usually followed by death. *Very* raised eyebrowish. I'm surprised the priest baptized you! Of course, yours must be a very intelligent family. Now mine are distinguished. When Quark and anti-Quark meet they annihilate each other and emit energy. We are a family of elementary particles.

KURU   I'm most honoured to hear your bedroom secrets.

QUARK   My particular family carried *great* weight. The three of us were known as the Baryons. Our cousins the Mesons interbred very weakly; and weakest of all, those of whom we scarcely speak, are the Gravitons. It's all in Debrett.

KURU   What of your Mother?

QUARK   She was an Overner. She did not come from the Isle of Wight. But in spite of a libidinous youth, we've all done well. The purple flowers of May's passion turn to transparent Honesty.

KURU   We had the whole medical profession against us; and the Church too. Only Cancer Research kept us going.

QUARK   An outside enemy heals family factions. (*Kuru paints her nails*) Nail remover? You'll be removing your hands in a moment. How's your boyfriend?

KURU   A worthwhile proposition.

QUARK   I don't trust him. In the same way that one does not trust a woman who has married into the peerage. Ah! the nubility! The marriage altar can be a guillotine to reputation.

KURU   One has to keep one's head in these matters.

QUARK   Indeed one does! Break his teeth with graven stones for me, will you? Society has to judge a woman by her sexual choice as it does a man by his job.

KURU   But I love my job. Snowy my trainer turned up at the side door in his green rolled-neck sweater and peaked cap, and said he'd brought his body to be buried. I was desperate in case someone saw it there, so I asked him to wait in the outhouse until I'd had time to find a dug patch of earth in the garden, a vegetable bed or something. I really wasn't sure if he should be wearing his sweater anyway if he was being buried, but I just couldn't bring myself to ask him to take it off.

QUARK   You were always individual. I remember my asking your mother to put your baby sister down on the floor. 'Let her have a little kick,' I said; and you proceeded to kick the baby.

KURU   My sister! She was the kind of woman who never hangs up her towel in the bathroom.

QUARK   Don't be unjust. Practice is only theoretical routine imposed by habit. In the end you grew past her. She used to play the slow movement of the Mozart like a cat with a saucer of cream.

KURU   She did have her good points, though she was pigeon-toed.

QUARK   Matching dichotomies are too easy to formulate. They save thought. You must develop the art of handling an argument to make a point that nobody can perceive. It silences them, and gains you an absolute advantage. Can you tell me why, when I'm at home, the water in my wash-basin rotates in a clockwise direction, but here it goes anti-clockwise? I must call the plumber. What's his name?

KURU   Coriolis. He's round and about a great deal. But we've missed the opportunity till tomorrow.

QUARK   Opportunity has a kiss-curl, but is bald at the back. In any case, it's bad medicine to prescribe a general remedy for a specific ill. I'm without income so must doctor my change.

KURU   Will you have a woman doctor?

QUARK   That is La grande peur des bien pensants. The panic reaction of conforming fools. Here. Take the grave of your fantasy (*Yields* KURU *the bath chair*) and put on my wig.

KURU   Time and chance happen to all. Ah, tranquillity! Old age is like a picture painted by an ex-husband. We love the art, but not the artist.

QUARK   Do you take your shoes off when you go to the theatre, when no one can see? They do pinch so.

KURU   (*Violently*) No! Gladness has been taxed. It's a dramatic conspiracy. Life-duties.

QUARK   Was your husband destroyed?

KURU   The medical report said 'After the divorce, the symptoms will clear up remarkably quickly when the damages are awarded.' (*Happy expression*) We had planned to have twins.

QUARK   Oh I'm not sure about twins. You can't lumber the changing-rooms of Europe with twins every time you go shopping for clothes. Anyway, when you've finished washing and changing one you have to start all over again with the other. Was it true of your aunt?

KURU   If you tell my aunt anything, she'll at once pretend she already knew rather than lower herself to admit she has learned anything from you. She lives a broad.

QUARK   There's something divinely wicked about going to Capri in January!

KURU   Let all things be done decently, and in order. I have a vision of a new and fertile land, now I am old. The bride with her sash, the wedding-songs and revelry, music in the hall, little ones! The laughter and the dancers. All I need now are life's simplicities, like sweet music from silver chimes. (*Pause*) Yet death creeps in on the old-age wedding reception. Mind the pothole!

QUARK   (*Pushing bath chair*) So sorry, Grandmama. It's a shell-cavity.

KURU   Go where you're looking!

QUARK   When they dig up the road I always feel a rush of sympathy for the earth. It smells so foul, as though it hated being cooped up under the hard surface, away from light and air all the time. And it looks so black.

KURU   Our decease will give it free aid. Waiting for you to push, Poussette, is like being furious with someone you thought was dead for putting you through the experience. Now, back to my vision. The bride stands there, shivering and tender. . . .

Exeunt, QUARK *as little girl pushing* KURU *as old woman.*

SCENE SEVEN

Music. KURU *and* QUARK *enter nude save for lavish coats made of feathers,* QUARK *in lighter coloured feathers,* KURU *if possible in Bird of Paradise feathers. The two coats must come up high behind the heads of the actresses to frame them, and have one button across the front to give form to the coat, but reveal nudity.*

The scene is a balletic cock-fight, a serious parody in mime against a background of music of the knife-fight of Scene Four.

SCENE EIGHT

Coat-stand upstage centre, with coats, behind which is hidden CHALONE. PHAGOCYTE *is upstage centre, back to audience, facing stand. He is stripped to his underpants, showing a severe and badly stitched scar across his back. Downstage of him, walking to and fro, is* SQUALOID, *swagger-stick in hand.* PHAGOCYTE *has arms outstretched at horizontal,* SQUALOID *clearly demanding that he keep them in that position however tiring.*

SQUALOID   You're the sort of person who's always looming small in the foreground. Aren't you! Eh? Answer me when I speak to you. (*Threatening*) Mind your head! (*Pause as* PHAGOCYTE *cringes*) I'm not going to hit you. Look at you with your shirt off. The doctors have stitched you up like a sheep. Disgusting. What a coward. One thing I really like about you

PHAGOCYTE   Let me go!

SQUALOID   is your running refrain. You never refrain and you're always running. Aren't you? Eh? One of those people who can only be objective when it doesn't concern them?

PHAGOCYTE   You're killing me!

SQUALOID   I haven't touched you! In the forces, anyway, fatality is accepted as part of the job in a way civilians don't understand. Fifty dead here has far less impact than it would in the home newspapers over breakfast.

PHAGOCYTE   Why are you doing this?

SQUALOID   You know damn well.

PHAGOCYTE   I'm sorry.

SQUALOID   That's it. Alternate song is what the muses love, as my old schoolmaster used to say. You're squealing nicely. What did you say?

PHAGOCYTE   I'm sorry. Let me go!

SQUALOID   Not before you tell me what you think of Chalone. He's been good to you, you're a friend of his, aren't you? But we don't like him. What do you say to that? Let's see your face. (*Peers round upstage at him*) You're like a beautiful woman whose gums show when she smiles. Now, what about Chalone?

PHAGOCYTE   He's a ruler who can't bear the sight of his own shadow.

SQUALOID   Good. More. Deny your master.

PHAGOCYTE   He became a general by default.

SQUALOID   Became a general by default, did he? Curled up in his protected status like a mouse in a codpiece, totally ineffective and pulling rank?

PHAGOCYTE   Yes.

SQUALOID   Go on. Say more. The reason you don't like distinctions drawn is because you're undistinguished. Yet you're a great one for giving yourself a spurious importance, bringing news to the mess of someone's death at every opportunity. How's the triumph of patience over bad temper getting on? Eh, Phagocyte?

PHAGOCYTE   It's unfair.

SQUALOID   It's an unfair world, Phagocyte. Remember what you've said about your leader? Now look who's here. Isn't that strange?
(CHALONE *moves coat-stand to one side to reveal his presence.* PHAGOCYTE *falls to the ground at the shock and remains motionless until end of scene.*)
And we haven't even touched you.

Exit SQUALOID *stage right*

CHALONE   (*To* PHAGOCYTE) Don't just wonder. Cherish a little understanding, too. In India once I saw a woman burying her children one after another like an open womb. Try to see what they feel.

Wedding bells loud and merry. Exit CHALONE *carrying coat-stand stage left. Enter* SQUALOID *stage right with large cross as for grave. Lighting casts long cruciform shadow as he places it beside* PHAGOCYTE'S *head. Exit* SQUALOID. *Wedding bells continue. Fade to black.*

SCENE NINE

Wedding bells blend into Fats Waller's 'Ain't misbe-havin''. Bells fade. Enter KURU *and* QUARK *in corsets, stockings and wide-brimmed hats on stilts, from stage left. Music fades.*

KURU   When did you last slit your wrists?

QUARK   (*Laughing*) You think like a man with one tooth trying to whistle.

KURU   This is like endlessly circling in an overfull car park.

QUARK   If this were my first time out, I *think* I could find my way home!

KURU   On these, speed equals distance, over-time. Have you the energy? Any battery for your assault? There's a bit of a money shortage.

QUARK   Why do men put us on stilts?

KURU   And treat us like whores? Because we're mantissae, objects to be multiplied on. All I ask is the veneer of sincerity. If I wasn't an exactress of cash I'd be dead. I can take money troubles, I can take sexual troubles, but the combination's a killer.

QUARK   I'm getting the hang of it. Are you? You're clever! I am learning humility, and perhaps a little gener-osity. The more I can learn to see myself as another person, the more I'm becoming able to act on that person's behalf.

KURU   You're right. Power should go to people who don't particularly want it.

QUARK   Then bishoprics should go to those who don't deserve them?

KURU   (*Descending from stilts*) Bishop-pricks? 'Course! As soon as a man is consecrated, to prevent the 'growth of Pride', he should at once go to a whore to empha-size that he will not change the way of life that led him to that holy calling. Continue to be a friend of sinners, weak as they are. Anyway, a bishop who's frustrated can't give his best to his job, and what higher calling is there than a bishop?

QUARK   Perhaps when they're that old the fire dies and desires decay.

KURU   But love is life's reason!

QUARK   Then that's how nature prepares us for death.

KURU   I was prepared for life by travelling on a football train. I was sitting in a compartment and in came six hooting fans. They mucked about, and I laughed with them, until they held me across their knees and played around till my bra was off. Then each had a feel with the blinds down. I didn't see a thing – could hardly breathe! Oh, they had a good look. And I was so scared I just giggled all the time. What a nit I was! I'd charge them now.

QUARK   (*Indicating* KURU's *falling shoulder-strap*) Mind your booby-trap.

KURU   Sex was shorn of its mystery for me – like a frightened boy who at last opens the door to the dark cupboard.

QUARK   Where are they?

KURU   Oh, you'll know them. They have the unmistakable walk of troops who've come through a bad time and are out for a good one. That's funny, though. Unless he's sent away, on leave he's as regular as a metronome.

QUARK   What's yours like?

KURU   He has a good brain. First class. Trouble is, it was put in backwards.

QUARK   Is he generous?

KURU   We'll soon find out. Equal pay will force every woman out to work. Rising prices will make the luxury of a kept housewife impossible. How's your grandmother?

QUARK   I'm terribly sorry to say she was kicked to death in a ladies' football match at Otmore two weeks ago. No, it's true!

KURU   (*Stifling her laugh. Knowingly.*) She knew what was in man. Was the set-up upset?

QUARK   I was.

KURU   What the eye doesn't see, the heart never, never grieves over. Never confess your affairs.

QUARK   What's the name of that man who's living with his wife? (*Sees men coming offstage right*) Oh! Is my hair all right? It's a bit oily.

           Enter from stage right SQUALOID *and* PHAGOCYTE *in loud suits and large bow-ties on pogo-sticks.*

KURU   No great sheiks. Cherry ripe?

           Having made dramatic entry bouncing in on their pogo-sticks they descend from them downstage right.

PHAGOCYTE Bath, Karl?

SQUALOID   I don't bath till I itch, Paul. I'm heartily relieved, after centuries of exploitation by women, at being excused from having to earn enough for two, three or four or five at a time. Breadwinning is a concept that's now thoroughly chaffed. What is a woman anyway but a generation gap?

PHAGOCYTE (*Seeing women*) My God, what's that?

SQUALOID   Merely two of them just indulging in whores' play.

PHAGOCYTE Très bonne affaire! Peace!

SQUALOID   Nice piece.

KURU   In this affair the wretched men are observing the speed limit. We will have to initiate. (*Mounting her stilts.* QUARK *has remained on hers throughout*)

QUARK   (*To the men*) How art thou fallen from Heaven!

KURU   Morning, son.

QUARK   Entertaining possibilities?

KURU   Is your priority propriety?

QUARK   (*Of* PHAGOCYTE) He looks very debonair.

KURU   Just come from a good nest, I'll be bound. Cadge a
            lift.

QUARK   He looks haggard.

PHAGOCYTE   (*To* SQUALOID) What a lure!

KURU   Hood him and seel his eyes.

QUARK   I'll call him Merlin, Merlin who rings up the sky-
            lark.

KURU   Oh, the impertinence of the 'phone. Merlin's a
            woman's bird! I'm becoming one at this rate. He
            looks disappointing; a gentle tassel. (*To* SQUALOID)
            Let me harmonize your affections with your reason
            and reconcile them with the interests of your senses.
            (*Wide-eyed to* QUARK) Ooo! His eyes are serpiginous,
            creeping from one part to the other!

SQUALOID   Women. Turn them upside down and they're all
            the same.

KURU   (*To* QUARK) No match for us? (*To* SQUALOID)
            Middle stump bold?

PHAGOCYTE   Interchangeable women.

KURU   What makes you think you're any good? Your
            inferiority complex?

QUARK   (*Charmingly, coming off stilts and moving her bottom
            seductively at* PHAGOCYTE) Why don't you draw a bow
            at a venture, my adventurous beau?

SQUALOID   (*Confidentially, to* PHAGOCYTE) Deb is bed, backwards.

KURU   (*To* SQUALOID) You're so small it would be dan-
            gerous to cut you down to size. (KURU *and* QUARK
            mount their stilts) He's the sort of man who rises
            between two stools.

SQUALOID   My father used to say 'Pour vinegar on them first. If they squeal, they've got V.D.'

QUARK   Oh dear. I would resign; only I don't want to appear a prima donna.

PHAGOCYTE   (*To* KURU *of* QUARK) Is she an Eskimo?

KURU   No. A Kabloona, like you.

SQUALOID   (*Taking* PHAGOCYTE *aside to teach him*) When duelling for another man's wife, be relaxed! Then she'll come to you, as all the pressure is from the other side.

QUARK   In matters of love, I expect you feel as I do. If it's got to happen, let's spin it out.

KURU   (*To men*) We're dichogamous. Self-fertilization is impossible.

SQUALOID   (*To* PHAGOCYTE) You have such a gift for making enemies I dread taking you out. (PHAGOCYTE *bounces on his pogo-stick*)

KURU   (*To* QUARK *of* PHAGOCYTE) Look at the intense personal struggle of one man!

PHAGOCYTE   (*Stopping. To* KURU) Tart is supposed to be sweet!

KURU   (*To* QUARK *of* SQUALOID) He's no better. I'm sick of making up in private for his public inadequacies.

QUARK   Be amiable.

KURU   (*To* SQUALOID, *seductively*) No interference?

SQUALOID   Only in (*thrusts his pogo-stick at her navel, startling her off her stilts*) naval engagements.

KURU   Rather un-Pauline behaviour!

SQUALOID   How's your friend Cloop?

KURU   Not Cloop. Quark.

PHAGOCYTE   (*Admiringly. As he speaks he punts towards* QUARK *with his pogo-stick as punt-pole*) Beautiful objects dictate their own peace; like a nude I saw punting in the sunshine on the Cambridge Backs.

QUARK   (*Coyly*) Oh you do have a warm imagination.

KURU   (*Fiercely, to* QUARK) Come on, pouting Caprice! (*To* PHAGOCYTE, *as though to put the idea into his head*) Your thoughts are running as wild as a camel on heat!

SQUALOID   (*To* PHAGOCYTE) If the stoic believes that pleasure must by definition be vicious . . .

PHAGOCYTE   (*To* SQUALOID) Then he must also believe that vice is the only pleasure. Come on!

KURU   (*Mounting stilts*) I'm wearing my blue shift, coming with velocity towards you! You won't live to observe it!

PHAGOCYTE   (*To* QUARK) Just say you looked at me, and saw me as young and fresh and electric, and said to yourself 'My word, I can't keep my hands off him; I'll put him to work in a trice.'

SQUALOID   (*To* PHAGOCYTE) You baboon!

QUARK   (*Circling* KURU *on her stilts*) A living dog is better than a dead lion, I suppose.

KURU   Always suspect flattery; then lean back and enjoy it.

SQUALOID   (*Holding* QUARK *still on her stilts with one hand while with the other describing three horseshoes in front of her body, one in front of each breast and one before crutch as he speaks*) Ever thought what the third horseshoe stands for in the pub sign?

QUARK   (*Descending from stilts.* KURU *descends at the same time*) He has all the insolence of a mirror in a landscape!

KURU   They have sex abnormalities. A normal male is XY. Female is XX. A male who is XXY is usually eunuchoid – underdeveloped internal and external genitalia – often of low I.Q. One who is XYY is often of exceptional height, with a serious personality disorder, this giving him an aggressive, anti-social and criminal tendency, ideal for the army.

PHAGOCYTE   (*Of* QUARK) There's a contained and sweet wildness about her.

          Bugle call offstage.

SQUALOID   (*Sharply at attention. Stamps foot*) Blue

PHAGOCYTE   (*Sharply at attention. Stamps foot*) Smoke

SQUALOID   (*Shoulders pogo-stick*) War

PHAGOCYTE   (*Shoulders pogo-stick*) White

SQUALOID   (*Turns off-stage right*) Bones

PHAGOCYTE   (*Turns off-stage right, behind him*) Men.

          SQUALOID *and* PHAGOCYTE *march off stage right.*

KURU   (*Contemptuously*) Tu! Fu!

QUARK   A confidence appalling in its sincerity!

KURU   (*Sing-song, after them*) So I must find a way to say farewell, (*Turning to* QUARK, *serious now, and prosaic*) although there is no other one but you.

QUARK   (*Disposing of stilts and hat offstage*) Look at the swallows carolling in the misty air!

KURU   (*Passing her stilts and hat to* QUARK *to be disposed of. Sighs*) Back to the royal craft of weaving.

QUARK   Lonely love makes me very selfish and inefficient. I *did* like the taller one.

KURU   All the garrulity of self-unconsciousness.

QUARK   He hardly spoke!

KURU   His spoke was hard. Perhaps we look too ordinary. There comes a point when dim lighting over your mirror ceases to be flattering and becomes plain foolhardy.

QUARK   I spend hours in the bathroom, reflecting in a mirror.

KURU   I've a new sort you must try. It eases tense (KURU *puts her hand on back of* QUARK'S *neck.* QUARK *stiffens rigid*) neck muscles.

QUARK   Love's a soft school. Night's broken up. The bell has gone for dawn.

SCENE TEN

Guillotine revealed upstage centre by KURU.

KURU   Kneel down here.

QUARK   (*Pause. Looks. Goes round behind it and places head in so that she faces the audience.*) Don't lock it.

KURU   Of course not. (*Locks it loudly with a snap*) Now that's interesting. The stalk's beak-mark usually fades during the first week of life – just above bridge of nose and back of neck at hair-line – but it's especially noticeable when baby cries. It proves baby comes on a stalk, doesn't it? Like a pod of peas!

QUARK   (*Whimpering*) What are you doing to me?

KURU   (*Going behind guillotine to begin undressing* QUARK) Bestiality is one thing, dear, but bedding plants really is a little beyond the pale. Pray!

QUARK   Let me out, let me out!

KURU   You have been found guilty of despair. Off with your pants.

          Head still fastened by guillotine, QUARK *has her clothes ripped off by* KURU, *leaving her pinned down and naked.*

QUARK   Oh give me heartsease if I'm going to die!

KURU   (*Beside guillotine, holding execution cord*) Shall I pull this string? Shall I? Shall I?

QUARK   (*Terrified*) No! Don't, don't, don't!

KURU   If we were both to agree, one of us might be wrong. They are giving the thumbs down, Quark darling. (*To audience*) Shall I, Ladies and Gentlemen?

QUARK   (*Hysterical*) I hate you I hate you I hate you! No! No!

KURU   You have five seconds more on earth. One, two, three, four, five.

          Blade descends. QUARK *screams. The guillotine is found to be harmless as blade strikes into wooden collar holding*

QUARK *down, but leaves her unharmed.* QUARK'S *expression moves from total terror to silent and gradual realization that* KURU *has not taken her life.* KURU *unlocks yoke.*

KURU *sits, downstage right.* QUARK *comes out from behind guillotine, naked, and dances for* KURU, *saying*

QUARK

The universe spins on a shaft of light
   Whose name is love.
Flowers of the meadows folded up all night
   Spread for high strength above
Them, warming out their secrets till
Displayed for all to see each world's a daffodil.

Full-blown with morning, laughing to the sky
   With puckered lips
They kiss sun's mastery to catch his eye.
   No night-jar trips
Among the undergrowth between the stars
For violets and primrose chain the bars.

I took a prism, dazzled as a king,
   And held it up.
Light shattered into all the flowers of spring.
   Kingcup
And stalked marsh-marigold, its spendthrift son,
Transfigured all around till night and day were one.

What vision have I seen? Flowers wheel like suns
   In daisy-chains of dance
Round daffodils, whose green-gold laughter stuns
   To ignorance
My day-dull thoughts. Then suddenly the clue
To all was clear. That source of light is you.

QUARK *looks at* KURU, *and moves slowly towards offstage left.*

KURU

(*Still sitting. Holds out her hand to* QUARK) Don't go.

QUARK *smiles and runs over to* KURU, *lies in her lap and sucks her breast as* KURU *says*

KURU Close, close tight buds, now parting ends the day
Laughter must cease
Colours fade, and withering winter come.
Yet say, even as you droop
And nod down to the roots from which you grow,
The shadows know
Even as they stretch their fingers on the lawn
No parting's loss when lovers long for dawn.

Seal up, sweet lids, the trembling of damp eyes
And glistening cheeks;
Strength is a beauty only known in grief:
Like men at war
Who find true comradeship in cruelty,
And bravery
Even as they mourn the very friends they kill –
So may this night of parting bind us still.

Fade on tableau to black.

END OF ACT ONE

Act Two

SCENE ONE

Siren, alert. Aircraft overhead, air-raid, then silence. SQUALOID *and* PHAGOCYTE *in urban foxhole.*

SQUALOID The city is going to fall. You got here safe?

PHAGOCYTE It's strangely quiet. There's that silent tenseness you feel when walking down a street where violence is about to break out.

SQUALOID It would help if we knew how much of our own army was on our side.

PHAGOCYTE It's like coming to work on Bank Holiday. I could hear my heels clicking along the empty streets, yet every move was watched. I could feel it.

SQUALOID Well here we are, stuck for a while. It's a good old soldier's rule: when you take up a new position or move into a new place – even if it's only for a short time – pretend to yourself you'll always be there and set about making it comfortable.

PHAGOCYTE Not many buildings left. I used to look at a cathedral, or at the Houses of Parliament, and think 'How massive! How indestructible! It'll surely last for ever!' Now I think 'One bang and it's flat. How fragile.'

SQUALOID I remember the first person I helped out of a doodlebug. We had to feel our way up the rubble. I was small so they said 'Go on, Tich!' and I felt her feet and shins. She had knitting on her lap and still had her glasses on the end of her nose. Covered in bricks. Dust and rubble. Funny how I remember her. Like my Mother's name.

PHAGOCYTE   Is this the time you long for a nine-to-five job; regularity, purpose?

SQUALOID   Are you mad? This is where purpose is. Saving your life. War's the ultimate test of manhood.

PHAGOCYTE   I hope not. (*Pause*) If we are taken, and interrogated, will you treat me as a friend?

SQUALOID   What the hell do you mean?

PHAGOCYTE   If they're going to torture me, kill me? I'm a coward if there's torture. It's a strong man who'll kill his friend at the friend's request, to save a movement in danger. (*Guns*)

SQUALOID   The guns have started! You bloody well hold on to hope. It's the only preservative. If you go about thinking of yourself as a martyr, you soon become one. Get that Bren and trim it.

PHAGOCYTE   What's this?

SQUALOID   Only human remains. Can you eat it?

PHAGOCYTE   No.

SQUALOID   Throw it to the moles and the bats. You'll learn. In Cambodia a squad shot and ate their paymaster when he'd no food to give them.

PHAGOCYTE   I feel sick as an arrested thief.

SQUALOID   You're useless. A great city has fallen before; a great city will fall again. (*Tank noise*) Hold your eyes bright!

PHAGOCYTE   It's a tank!

SQUALOID   Can't be ours. Give me the bazooka, quick. Don't know who's on what side in this war. They're checking each one of us in turn. For Christ's sake don't stand behind! (*BANG*)

PHAGOCYTE   That's a direct hit. Hideous.

SQUALOID   Basic military strategy, Fire and Movement. Tanks always fight in threes. Watch for the other two. Four men are incinerating in that molten mess at this moment.

PHAGOCYTE   There's nowhere to go!

SQUALOID   It's everyone for himself now. The embassies have closed, the rats have left – even the brothels are shut.

PHAGOCYTE   All the shops along the streets are planked with thick boards.

SQUALOID   You can bet your mother's belly-button the brass-hats have jumped. There's no such thing as politics. Only politicians. And I hate them as vermin.

PHAGOCYTE   It must have been a rogue tank. On my way I stopped to catch my breath for a moment under the eaves of a house, and a beautiful local woman empties a chamberpot all over me.

SQUALOID   You're going to say it's ruddy Eve's dropping next. Keep your mind on survival, will you? Victories can't be counted before the last battle.

PHAGOCYTE   Technology's given us the power of gods, yet turned us into beasts.

SQUALOID   Look, you fool, the only answer to raw nature, which is what we have here, is the rigid hierarchy of the army. And now that's gone. The city is being taken in a pincer. Sapper units have infiltrated along with the refugees from the countryside, and now we're surrounded by tanks. There'll be no surrender of weapons in this war. It's starvation.

PHAGOCYTE   The harvest's over and ungathered.

SQUALOID   Burned with flame-throwers. Your skin goes black like an oven with famine. When elected authority begins to crumble, and the army's been infiltrated, people make their own compromises with whatever authority's on the streets. Self-interest's a damn sight more use now than honourable bravery.

PHAGOCYTE   You're a born survivor.

SQUALOID   That's why I'm here, isn't it?

PHAGOCYTE   (*As* KURU *enters with* QUARK, *drab clothes*) What's that, refugees? We used to speed over open ground to reach the safety of the next city. Now we'd be more sensible if we fled the cities for the wild.

SQUALOID   It's a woman, carrying something. War makes ordinary people do extraordinary things. What's *she* doing out?

Sounds of distant heavy machine-gun fire.

KURU   (*Sings*) Sleep, my little one. Hush!
The guns chatter all night,
Their flames are lively.
Sleep, my little one,
Soon you'll grow up and play with them.
Hush, it is nothing, my little love,
Close your ears, sleep, sleep,
It's nothing, just life.

They leave. Sounds of street-fighting.

PHAGOCYTE   (*Looking through trench telescope*) The tanks are in the streets! It's door-to-door shooting. Further away the lampposts have men hanging from them! It's not dung on that field, it's a pile of dead. Oh God!

SQUALOID   They'll come here when they see the tank. Have your knife ready and check the weapons. Here.

PHAGOCYTE   We're totally without cover.

SQUALOID   I'll cut your throat as an act of mercy if you don't help yourself.

Sounds of street-fighting.

PHAGOCYTE   They've shot that old man!

SQUALOID   He's well and truly in the mud. It'll be a long time before he gets up again.

PHAGOCYTE   How strong's this foxhole?

SQUALOID   About as trustworthy as old age in a bootlace. (*Shell explodes*) Duck! All that's left of this city is its eyes to weep. I warn you, they've a nasty habit in this place. Some of our men woke up in the morning totally and permanently paralysed. Someone in the night had shoved a bicycle spoke in a key place and punctured their backbones. Hardly a mark. (*Pause*) I'd sooner be dead. Sleep with your back against something that can't have a spoke pushed through it.

PHAGOCYTE   I've seen no children in the streets since we came. The squares are empty.

SQUALOID   In battle one only thinks of women in the context of a hole. Duck!

Aeroplane takes off overhead.

PHAGOCYTE   Don't fire! It's refugees!

SQUALOID   Like hell it is. Look at those men hanging on to the undercarriage, the wheels!

PHAGOCYTE   God! He's dropped. They've napalmed the streets! A sheet of flame. Someone's firing a mortar at it!

SQUALOID   One of those who didn't get on, I expect.

PHAGOCYTE   It's lurching, it'll come down!

SQUALOID   I doubt it. There must be five or six people in every set of three seats. What a weight! Like an old whale trying to get airborne. It's done it though!

PHAGOCYTE   That was for women and children! I despise my kind.

SQUALOID   Don't complain. Next time it'll be you. The ones who survive look after themselves. You can weep later. (*Sounds of street-fighting*) If you go that way the flame-throwers will get you. If you go that, the tanks are waiting. All we need now are the bombs.

PHAGOCYTE   Those are two of our own men, creeping across the bodies; they're looting! (*Raises his rifle to shoot them*)

SQUALOID (*Preventing him*) Leave them. Famine makes savages.

PHAGOCYTE Christ send another ceasefire!

SQUALOID Ceasefires are just springboards for advances. There'll be no more till the city's lost. I'll tell you something. I was taken prisoner once with a patrol. I felt the same then. No fear. I suppose battle-anger stifles fear. The supreme cold-blooded test is staying sane day after day under heavy direct mortar fire without leaving the foxhole. Mind out!

Mortar fire.

We were lined up against a wall with machine-guns trained on us, but were so wet we didn't really care what happened. I suppose we did deep down, but I had a feeling the whole thing was unreal. We'd not eaten, had no sleep. We were at rock bottom. That's what saved us, that feeling. If just one of us had panicked, or fought back or run, all of us would have been mowed down.

PHAGOCYTE What a pageant of futility!

SQUALOID Think of Warsaw. It's a mystery, man's ability to build again. (*Tank noise*) The second tank! Stand aside. (*Fires bazooka*) If the bombers come over we've one Sam-seven hand-held that will bring a few of them down. Red sky in the morning. All that matters now is luck.

Bombing and blackout.

SCENE TWO

KURU *and* QUARK, *dressed as for opening of Act One, Scene Nine* (*but without stilts or hats*), *enter and cross the stage, laughing hysterically.*

SCENE THREE

Dark stage. Enter SQUALOID, *with lantern. Then to him* CHALONE, *dressed as officer.*

CHALONE   You've made it. Where's Phagocyte?

SQUALOID   He's alive somewhere.

CHALONE   We don't trust him. He has not been told the code, but we believe he may know it. If he knows it he's with the suborned wing. See if you can find out, when the chance comes. The code is Peas in pod.

SQUALOID   Urine and pregnancy?

CHALONE   Yes. No more, now. In war, as in marriage, never tell more than the other person needs to know. Goodnight.

         Exit CHALONE. *Enter* PHAGOCYTE, *with lantern.*

SQUALOID   Luck held?

PHAGOCYTE   War seems to take the good men, not the bad. I've lost my oldest friend.

SQUALOID   Who?

PHAGOCYTE   Gaba.

SQUALOID   Zylo went too; and Gamahuche.

PHAGOCYTE   If war is about anything positive it's about comradeship. I had a feeling I'd suffered a physical hurt. My reason was stunned, though I wasn't touched. Just at the mercy of fear.

SQUALOID   Why do they allow men like you in the army?

PHAGOCYTE   Please remember what we said. If I'm taken, and they're going to break me, kill me. It's the office of a friend.

SQUALOID   There's a telegram for you. (*Hands him telegram*)

PHAGOCYTE   (*Opens it*) I've had a son. Death's an horrific commonplace; but birth is still a miracle.

SQUALOID   Hobbies are a complete bore if you don't share them.

PHAGOCYTE   You used to be one-sided in your opinions, but now there's a pretty even imbalance.

SQUALOID   Here's some brandy. Congratulations. (*Cleaning

chunks of mud off his shoes) There's something deeply satisfying about cleaning your own shoes.

PHAGOCYTE   (*Taking a swig*) Mud in your eye! Where are the officers?

SQUALOID   The lunatics have taken over the asylum. They should know better how to run it.

PHAGOCYTE   Are you welshing on me?

SQUALOID   (*Affably*) Pure music, bach. I hide an idea you handled that Mozartfully.

PHAGOCYTE   Do you see evil in war?

SQUALOID   Only vile bodies. (*Mortar fire*) Oh for the bright swiftness of hand-to-hand combat instead of these random mortars! The officers? Most rule depends on a right judgement of other people's judgement. That's all that matters, really. And ours get it wrong each time.

PHAGOCYTE   Your understanding passes all peace.

SQUALOID   I can tell you. Some of my capital of resilience has been permanently used up. You only have a certain amount. The main enemy is this mud. Clean your rifle. There's nothing dishonourable about a weapon.

PHAGOCYTE   Don't forget what we've agreed, if we're taken.

SQUALOID   For Christ's sake! We won't be taken. There's a lull, and it'll last a day or two now the city's fallen, till they sort out who's in charge. Pass the time. Avoid a void.

PHAGOCYTE   I'll sleep.

Swift fade to black.

SCENE FOUR

Upstage centre, bright red English pillar-pox.

Enter SQUALOID *with rifle at alert, searches around. When satisfied that no one is near, stands rifle against pillar-box, goes round behind it and pretends to urinate against it. Comes round downstage of box and picks up rifle again. Searches for possible enemies as before. Then takes a peach-stone out of his mouth and posts it as though it were a letter. Knocks on pillar-box.*

SQUALOID   You there?

KURU *emerges from pillar-box dressed in transparent mackintosh, through which shows her bright red underwear.*

KURU   (*In French accent*) You needn't have posted your spit-out.

SQUALOID   (*As* KURU *adjusts her bra-strap*) Playing on your bra's band?

KURU   (*French accent as before*) I'm not your french letter from a broad! Object to the colour? (*Showing strap*) I'm not wearing dark knickers, even if they have given an order that all places of entertainment must be blacked out. Hard up?

SQUALOID   (*Pinches her bottom*) No hard feelings!

KURU   (*Drops the French accent*) I don't think you know what it is to be totally destitute without any money at all. To know you'll have to search for hours to find anyone to employ you for immediate cash, and then to have to work and wait hours again before the cash is paid you, and you can buy a full meal.

SQUALOID   True of men. Women can always sell crumpet.

KURU   If you think of me as property, I'm lost.

SQUALOID   Met your Waterloo, have you? We'll call you Victoria! When I went back to France I saw Madam Claude and I screwed her free, and she said if ever I wanted a bird she'd let me have one without paying.

KURU   You men all have to build up your egos the same way. But you've me! I'll be yours alone, if you'll look after me.

SQUALOID   Right. Are you clean? If you caught V.D.! Oh,

gonorrhoea was the worst. They'd prize open the hole of your penis (*Looking down rifle-barrel*), and look down it and search around, and then the medic would pour permanganate of potash in to scour out the disease. (*Grimaces*) It would be a long time before a man would want to risk having that done to him again.

KURU   (*Close to him, stroking him*) Do you know what my secret and pet name for your penis is? Your eel. I've never told anyone before. That's what I think of when I stroke it.

SQUALOID   (*Starts. Moves away*) Do you mind? Has a man no privacy even in public? The little boys at the transport depot would run out and say 'You jig-a-jig my sister? Very cheap?' Jesus! they were dirty.

KURU   So would you be after fifty men a night, one after the other, five minutes each.

SQUALOID   Sure. The Colonel said 'Do you know, I've just seen half my regiment queuing up at the local brothel!' He didn't know I'd just come from there. I tried, but I couldn't. She was so scrubby.

KURU   Well, I'm not, and I give you my promise it will be you and no one else.

SQUALOID   What's your little friend like?

KURU   Quark? She's like a bird. The day or two before her man comes back from abroad she talks to herself, quietly, non-stop, in her room; sometimes in her mirror – she's hundreds of mirrors, a whole collection of them – sometimes to her teddy-bears, chirruping away for up to six hours at a time, hovering around her kitchen and bedroom. He's her sun, she sings for him. But the war's ended all that.

SQUALOID   Gives a clean sweep. Come on. We've a crematorium service for Gaba, Gamahuche and Zylo. You mourn, I'll deal with the coffins. It's due to begin.

          Exeunt.

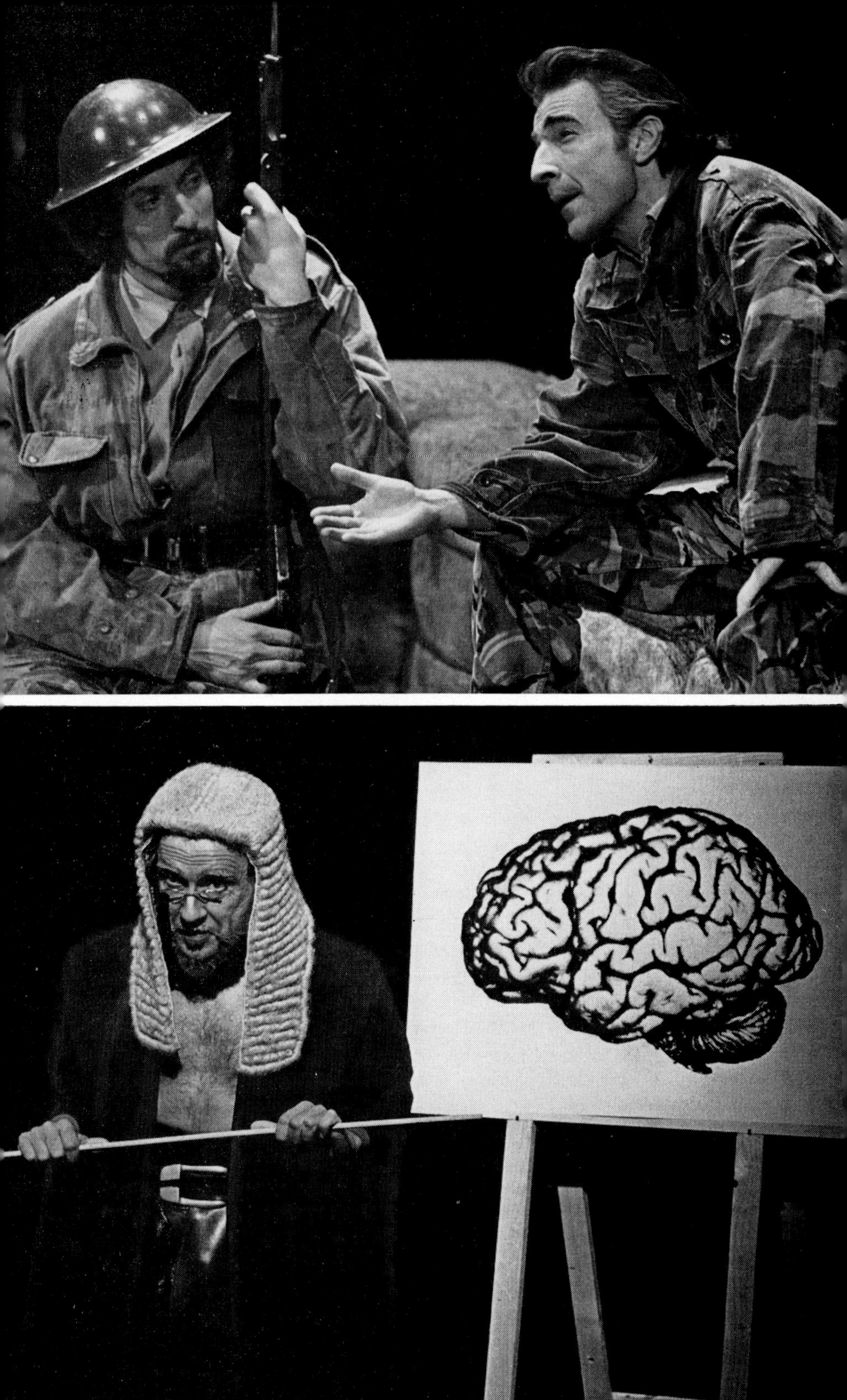

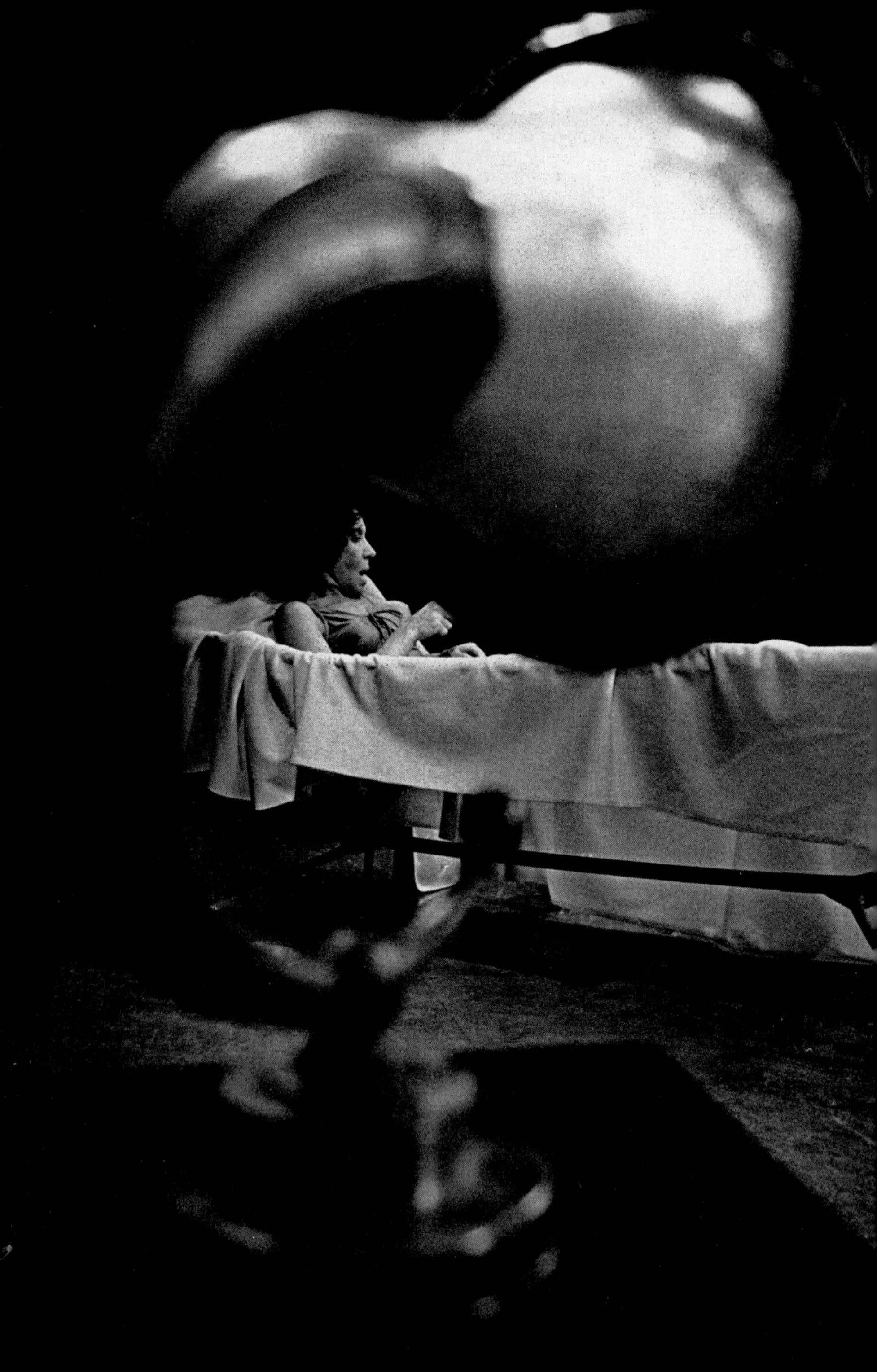

SCENE FIVE

Introit, 'Requiem aeternam' from Roland de Lassus Requiem for Five Voices begins. Once established, mix in distant gunfire.

Upstage right fire-bucket, red, with word 'Fire' facing audience. Beside it, on the offstage side of it, will be placed the six dead bodies. Red spotlight on this area, as for flames.

PHAGOCYTE and KURU upstage left as though attending church service, PHAGOCYTE in shirtsleeves (army issue), KURU in black, with large pink heart on downstage (left) arm-sleeve.

CHALONE dressed as priest for the taking of the service, downstage left of centre, vast prayer-book in hands from which he reads.

CHALONE   Lord, let something remain.

During the following readings, SQUALOID, stripped to waist, wearing white apron, from stage left pushes in open coffin on low castors in which is a dead body. When centre-stage he halts; goes round upstage centre of the coffin, genuflects reverentially first time, but with increasing speed with each subsequent corpse so that by the sixth the whole ritual is grossly perfunctory. Then lifts out corpse and places it beside fire bucket. By the end of the scene there is a pile of six dead bodies, final one with rope around neck, in a heap under the red light.

Abroad the sword bereaveth, at home there is as death. Lamentations, one, twenty.

It is a time of suffering for God Himself, who must destroy his own creation.

Destruction upon destruction is cried; for the whole land is spoiled. Jeremiah, four, twenty.

Is this the city that men call The Perfection of Beauty, The Joy of the whole Earth? Lamentations, two, fifteen.

There is no man that hath power over the spirit to

retain the spirit; neither hath he power in the day of death. Ecclesiastes, eight, eight.

Will you sit for the lesson? If gunfire comes closer, please crouch under your benches.

From Jeremiah forty-eight and forty-nine. Fear, and the pit, and the snare shall be upon thee. He that fleeth from the fear shall fall into the pit; and he that getteth up out of the pit shall be taken in the snare. If the grape gatherers come to thee, would they not leave some gleaning grapes? If thieves by night, they will destroy till they have enough. But I have made Esau bare: his seed is spoiled. All the cities thereof shall be perpetual wastes. Howl and cry; tell ye it in Arnon, that Moab is spoiled.

On the word 'Friends' SQUALOID, *who has obviously done this many times before, stops and bows head, hands pressed in attitude of prayer, until the brief sermon is over and he can continue his work.*

Friends, our brothers are brought to rest today in torment and violence, and all are eaten with famine. I would simply remind you it has all happened before.

SQUALOID *pushes coffin off stage left again to collect sixth (final) corpse.*

Two Kings, six, twenty-eight and twenty-nine. And the King said unto her, What aileth thee? And she answered, This woman said unto me, Give thy son, that we may eat him today, and we will eat my son tomorrow. So we boiled my son, and did eat him: and I said unto her on the next day, Give thy son, that we may eat him: and she hath hid her son.

Jeremiah, five, eight. They were as fed horses in the morning: everyone neighed after his neighbour's wife.

Exit SQUALOID, *his work completed, stage left, pushing empty coffin before him.*

Let us pray. Let us renounce the vain pomp and glory of the world, with all covetous desires of the same, and the carnal desires of the flesh, and throw ourselves on His infinite mercy.

Directly addressing audience.

In the kingdom of light are many rivers. While we linger and tarry on earth the hour of our going, whether it is at midnight or in the morning, is of no moment in the dazzling eyes of God.

Exit CHALONE

SCENE SIX

KURU *seizes* PHAGOCYTE's *hand, to his astonishment, and drags him downstage.*

KURU   Give me life! Give me life! Hold my hand, hug me!

PHAGOCYTE   This is an appalling shock to morale.

KURU   I'm your new horizon! Anything's better than that dust down the throat. Let me feel alive again! When a chick breaks the eggshell, it comes out chirping as loud as it can. I can't stand all this death!

PHAGOCYTE   We need people with your vitality in the hospitals. There ought to be a cross-section of ages in the geriatric wards. After a life-time of privacy, the old dears are suddenly herded together, and all equally vulnerable. You only need one bullying nurse. The other patients won't dare stick up for the one being mocked, in case it's their turn next. When one of them asks for a bed-pan, the nurse might be tired, or just bloody-minded, and say 'Oh, you can wait!', and put her through agonies. Then, when she does on occasion have an accident, the nurse may well say, as a joke, 'Oh you dirty old woman!' But the joke to the nurse is a wound to the dignity of the old woman. More horror goes on in hospital than in many a prison cell.

KURU   For God's sake forget hospitals and death and prisons! I need nature, and love.

PHAGOCYTE   Ah! Now there I'm with you. It's lambing-time at home. There's life for you. Birth. If you're lambing a ewe, you can expect one, or twins, but three is a lot; and by the third the ewe is not expecting another. True, three slip out more easily, but she's tired and distracted and hasn't the strength to clean it, so it can smother if you're not there to help.

KURU   To my horror my stomach started to rumble in the middle of prayers. Everyone thought it was the telephone.

PHAGOCYTE   I hate funerals. In Egypt I was asked, would I take charge of forty civilian labourers with baggy trousers. I was one engineer with forty labourers, so they weren't going to learn English. I was with them all day, so there was no option. I picked up 'laazim' – means 'I want'; 'shaakoosh' means 'hammer'. You should say 'aywa' if you mean 'yes', or 'imshi! imshi!' if you mean 'Go away!' 'Iggri' if you want to say 'quickly' . . .

KURU   Oh, iggery, ae-ya-wa, iggery, iggery!

PHAGOCYTE   I had their respect because I prayed with them. Three times a day, arse in the air. They called me (*With deep pride*) Abbu Staff. Never called any other Staff Officer that. Trouble is, (*Thoughtfully*) if you're a Mohammedan, you can't say your prayers in an English airport toilet as the back of your head shows underneath the door. You'd look daft. It's a very real problem.

KURU   But you're not a Mohammedan, are you?

PHAGOCYTE   Look, have you seen *my* head under a lavatory door? Well then of course I'm not. (KURU *rips open her dress to expose herself*) What are you doing?

KURU   I've already said 'Quickly, yes, quickly, quickly'; how much clearer do I have to make it? (*Taking him by the hand and dragging him off*) Oh come on!

PHAGOCYTE   (*Puzzled*) Bloody funny funeral, this.

               Exeunt.

SCENE SEVEN

Garden scene. QUARK *in two-piece bathing costume stage right swinging on swing,* KURU *in one-piece bathing costume in hammock stage left, podding peas. Between them is an old-style gramophone, with horn.*

QUARK   In Doncaster they make it into blancmange.

KURU   (*Laughing*) Even if we have fallen in love, let's remain good friends.

QUARK   I hid from you when you arrived as I was afraid of myself. Then when you joined us on the bus, you had the choice of sitting next to Meson or me. I hoped and prayed you would sit by her, as I didn't want to be upset and disturbed just now. It's something about your eyes. It must be magic. You're laughing at me!

KURU   I'll lose my laughter when I lose my shadow!

QUARK   (*Running over to her and taking her hand*) Am I your shadow? I can be sad, even in laughter.

KURU   You were in love with Phagocyte.

QUARK   Oh *him*. Now I love you.

KURU   Every rich character has a vein of negativity in him. Cowardice is his.

QUARK   (*Swings*) Isn't this lovely! With you I feel all predy.

KURU   Predy?

QUARK   With decks stripped and ready for action. Tell me about your last husband.

KURU   He was a good wife. Don't let's talk about him. He committed suicide on our second honeymoon. I must have upset him.

QUARK   Because of your first husband?

KURU   Once you've broken with someone, there's an awful
            feeling of softness for them afterwards.

QUARK   What a life of change!

KURU   Change of life. Yes. My first husband was unfaithful
            first. *She* was someone else's mistress. My man came
            in drunk one evening while she was staying with us,
            and he made a pass at her. She laughed him away
            and said, 'I don't believe in incest', and all was well.
            He kept a diary, though; naturally I read it. Instead
            of being cross with him and grateful to her, I was
            furious with her! (*Pause*) I always like to see my
            husbands in the best possible light.

QUARK   Incest's only a relative proposition. If you really love
            somebody, you love them wholly, with all their
            faults and adulteries. Men don't understand that.
            It doesn't change.

KURU   Sometimes it does, darling. The pearl of sex is not
            in your cherry but in the mind. (*Producing a photo-
            graph from her handbag*) There he is! Look at that
            handwriting. I know you can't read it, but what
            character! What decisive and firm certainty! And
            look at that face. No, not conventionally good-
            looking, but what a clear and defined, a complete
            person looks out at you. That broken nose and
            shaved head. No, I mean it.

QUARK   (*Laughing*) It's marvellous to be in love.

KURU   Sickening. The need to be alone when he's away.
            Able to think of nothing else, do nothing else, wake
            elated at four in the morning and burst into tears at
            six in the evening. Write endless scribbles, and hang
            about the 'phone, hardly daring to have a bath in
            case the noise of the water drowns the 'phone if
            he rings. Talking to yourself. Imagining the worst of
            what's happening to him while he's away. Going to
            bed early and staring at the ceiling. Reliving every
            detail of shared experiences, believing every separa-
            tion is the final disaster. Eagerness of anticipation,
            and catastrophic depression when a date is post-

poned. Refusal to 'phone anyone else, especially of the opposite sex, to keep mentally uncontaminated. Is that his foot on the stair? Is that his car outside? Hours spent at the window.

QUARK   Did you feel like that when you were married?

KURU   My first marriage? Oh, he'd say, 'You're a married woman and housewife of thirty and should behave like it.' But I didn't feel like that, I'm not that kind of respectable. I didn't want to be wishing my youth away. He never made me feel young. If I did go out, he always demanded I made love to him when I came in. If I wouldn't he'd say, 'Oh, I suppose you've had it already this evening.' It was so degrading! But when I had the curse he slipped off to Wales. If he had allowed me my freedom I wouldn't have wanted to be unfaithful. (*Pause*) Not so often.

QUARK   How did it break up?

KURU   Tie my legs up and I'll tell you. I'm getting all excited, I don't know why. (QUARK *ties* KURU'*s legs together with a large ribbon in a bow*) I think I'm beginning to like the idea of being watched by, but not granting it to, a voyeur. There's power!

QUARK   Wishful thinking can be its own reward. (*Shyly*) I tie myself up with excitement when I'm alone.

KURU   You know, Quark, I'm feeling very guilty.

QUARK   About your marriage?

KURU   I had a secret. Like the childhood tree-house. I could be alone in the middle of London, able to go in any direction I wanted, and no one knew where I was. My husband didn't get in till late. I'd set off for home from work at five thirty, and just drop in on our secret love-nest for a quick gin and-tonic for a couple of hours. Then one day I turned up and there was only the telephone on the bare floorboards in the middle of an empty room.

QUARK   Some lover!

KURU   And my husband knew all the time! So, it was divorce by mutual dissent. (*With relish*) As he got older his left ear heard everything a semitone higher than his right.

QUARK   What a terrible fate!

KURU   Imagine listening to Wagner!

QUARK   Music's fall. My father was very good to my mother. Did you know that my uncle was a monk?

KURU   A monk! (*Untying her legs*) He must have had a bottomless passion for being hard up. I met my ex-husband last Monday and he was calm. Most irritating. It was like going to shut a door that wasn't there. No anger or anything. Nothing to hit against. I couldn't even bring myself to be angry with myself.

QUARK   You should never ask of a person emotionally more than he is prepared to give.

KURU   (*Philosophically*) All you need for marriage is to put on weight and throw it about. I've always thought of rules as guidelines, sensible suggestions for others, to tell you how they'll behave. For that I'm grateful. I've never thought of them as applying to me.

QUARK   At school I hated rules. I was in the middle of Middle Infants. Not Bottom Juniors, as my cousin Meson was. She called herself a Junior, but she was really Bottom Juniors. You leave when you are in Top Juniors.

KURU   This is worse than Lance-Corporal, Corporal, three stripes, Staff Sergeant, Warrant Officer Two, and R.S.M. with scrambled egg! I haven't mentioned the Commissioned Ranks; don't suppose they come in the lower school.

QUARK   I cried because I never ate sweets as I was saving my teeth, and they accused me of stealing sweets during playtime.

KURU   (QUARK *looking through* KURU's *handbag behind* KURU's *back*) After an emotional crisis a man can go back to his poker-game, but the woman is left alone, even by her best girl-friend. In fact, if you had a good man and she'd a chance of stealing him from you, she'd happily betray you.

QUARK   I've been looking at your wedding photos. One is always so busy looking radiant.

KURU   It takes a woman to understand our fear of dependence on men.

QUARK   Lie back and I'll tell you a story. (*Swinging*) Once all the stars had a meeting to see what they could do to brighten the earth. One small one volunteered to risk being a shooting star when the sun was looking the other way. She survived the journey, but became very small, as bits of her were blown away as she rushed through the sky. The sun saw her at the last minute and ... (*Gunfire*) What's that?

KURU   Do you sleep all day like an astronomer? That's the guns.

QUARK   What's going to happen?

KURU   Now we see in a fortune-teller's crystal cloudily, but eventually we'll find out face to face.

QUARK   Is there real danger?

KURU   You'll be taken for a bride.

QUARK   (*Laughing*) That's a penetrating thought!

KURU   Stand up for truth!

QUARK   Fallen, we lie. Was your last husband beautiful?

KURU   The reigning son.

                Gunfire.

QUARK   Again!

KURU   It's so like men. They make a society based on fear;

fear of breakdown of law and of outside enemies. Create an army with a rigid hierarchy that cultivates death as a means of enforcement. This leads to war, and so to the collapse of the very society that had created it for its own protection!

QUARK   But need it affect us?

KURU   Of course! (*With relish*) The sexual urge forces us to mate, so the next generation will be born. This is strait-jacketed into marriage, society's tolerance of sex in a limited context. But you can't damn up natural forces like that, so what happens? Sex outside becomes disruptive and illegal, divorced from society, this leads to exploitation, and violence, and so the police, then the army come in. That's why I love soldiers. That's why I'm guilty. Do you like men in uniform?

QUARK   Guilty? But surely that was during your marriage! It's not fornication if you're married, only adultery.

KURU   I'm not talking about that. (*Pause*) I went back with Phagocyte.

QUARK   What? At the cremation? I thought you were in love with me! I would have done anything you wanted. And with him! You cat! You linsang!

KURU   He gave me these peas I'm podding! Said it was our secret code, what he'd like to do to me. I was so low, and sick of all this death and depression and destruction and mourning and anyway it was a warm day and my most randy time of the month and I just felt I had to affirm life at once then and there. Anyway, Phagocyte's always attracted me.

QUARK   (*Doing physical exercise 'jerk and fling' with her arms in an effort to keep her temper*)

I must, I must
Increase my bust
Because it's best
For my chest.

KURU   And what made it worse was I'd just promised
           Squaloid I'd sleep only with him from now on: and
           an hour later I was carried away.

QUARK   When you think of a chicken laying an egg, (*Implying*
           KURU) and you think of a quail, (*Implying herself*)
           you've more respect for the quail.

KURU   Oh I know you're far better. I'm sorry.

QUARK   (*Forgiving. Standing on swing and swinging*) Look! I am
           a weight that can be picked up with five fingers!

KURU   I'm fed up with myself. I'm getting all the weary
           knowingness of the happily married housewife.

QUARK   I love the smell of freshly split peas in pod. Were you
           a great quarreller? A real warmonger?

KURU   I found the man who shouts you down may well be
           influenced by what you said, so used to get in first to
           make sure. (QUARK's *swing spins round*) You're spin-
           ning like a sycamore.

QUARK   The ground's shaking!

KURU   The guns are nearer.

QUARK   Remember, the best defence against rape is to go
           for his crutch.

KURU   Don't be mad! Give in, and you might survive. Give
           him a good time so he wants to keep you alive for
           more. In war nothing else works.

QUARK   The trees are full of tears. There are flames! It's
           dark. What's happening? The stars are too fright-
           ened of these flowers of light.

           Lights dimming.

KURU   The stars give out light, that's why you can see them;
           but the black hole of war sucks in everything, even
           light itself. Let's run.

           *They take hands and exeunt. Lights down to black. In-
           creasing gunfire.*

SCENE EIGHT

Lighting should now emphasize the fact that the full stage is and has throughout the play been a human brain in which and in front of which the action takes place.

Gunfire fades into sound of marching feet. They halt.

SQUALOID *in shirtsleeves, army issue, with Stirling sub-machine-gun slung from shoulder, playing darts stage left of centre against a dartboard on which has been pinned a centre-page spread nude from magazine such as 'Penthouse'.*

KURU *leads in* QUARK *to* SQUALOID *from stage right.* KURU *is dressed in bathing costume as in previous scene, over which she now wears a yellow beach-gown.* QUARK *in bikini as in previous scene.*

QUARK   What are you going to do?

SQUALOID   (*Throwing dart*) Just spend a little time with you.

QUARK   (*Cheerfully*) I saw a bear at the bottom of the garden.

KURU   Now you're a very naughty child; that's a lie. You must not tell lies like that. It's not clever. I'll have you beaten for telling lies. I don't like it. You're a wicked girl.

QUARK   (*Near to tears*) Well, I *nearly* saw a bear, then.

SQUALOID   Where was she this afternoon?

QUARK   (*Confidentially*) They forced me to lie nude in bed with a wounded man. It was a horrible shock when he tried to make love to me, and died!

SQUALOID   Is she easy?

KURU   Her generosity springs from her insecurity.

QUARK   (*Cheerfully. Skipping without a rope*)
            Girls are elastic
            Boys are fantastic . . .

SQUALOID   Now listen, little one. Will you tell us what you know?

QUARK Yes, I'll confess. (*Pause*) I was in Ireland – you know how trusting the people are there – and a couple I knew slightly were going away for a holiday. I said I'd look after the baby to give them a break. They needed it. It was only for two weeks. I said I'd be there in time for them to catch the bus from their village, the next village to ours. There was only one bus each afternoon, so they gave baby his tea and left him strapped in his high chair. But they hadn't confirmed it. It was all rather vague. I forgot. (*Pause*) When they came back a fortnight later, baby was still in his chair. (*Whispering, wide-eyed*) The mother went insane! (*Radiant chuckle*)

KURU Sweet Jesus!

QUARK My father was killed by a halo of bees. They never told me at the time.

SQUALOID Her superego's been lobotomized.

QUARK Yes. The queen bee kills those who mate with her. Bees know you by your voice, you should always talk to them. But they change their character after dark. My father had been making hay all day, so the adrenalin in his blood was high. Just before midnight he thought he'd take a walk down to the hives to see how they were, forgetting you shouldn't visit them by night. They swarmed him. Mother woke at five and found he wasn't beside her and went to look for him. He was face down in the vegetables. (*Pause*) At the funeral they told me he'd died of a heart attack, so I wouldn't be upset.

KURU Do you think about death?

QUARK Death? It's like going up a long flight of stairs, and turning out the light at the top. Pitch darkness. Then out through the door into the open air, a dimly lit nightworld we've no control over.

SQUALOID (*Good-humouredly, a whim*) Would you deny there's a God?

QUARK   I can't say I've given it much thought. (*Pause*) But I'm sure He's there!

SQUALOID   Will you say there's no such thing as God if we let you go?

QUARK   (*Pause*) I can't.

SQUALOID   Even with pain facing you?

QUARK   My birthday's February 2nd, Candlemas. Snowdrops are emblems of the Feast of Lights!

SQUALOID   She's nuts. Come on, help me give her the treatment.

QUARK   The infant daisies in January down by the river are so small in the grass they look like the remains of frost.

SQUALOID   Oh, shut her up! (*To* QUARK, *as he extracts darts from dartboard*) We'll make your head like a weasel-sucked egg.

KURU   What are you going to do to her?

SQUALOID   See.

KURU   Why?

SQUALOID   To find out what she knows and how she knew it.

KURU   (*With rising panic*) But she's a child!

SQUALOID   Look, the city's fallen. This isn't a holiday camp!

QUARK   Is my cat all right?

SQUALOID   It's been eaten. There's no food.

QUARK   ⎫   No! No!
⎬ *Together*
KURU   ⎭   Why?

SQUALOID   You women! (*Throws dart viciously at nude on board*) You don't care who's hurt provided your cat's safe! You make me hate. (*Throws second dart*) We can use the electrics, or take the toe off.

KURU   No, I won't bear it! It's not fair.

SQUALOID   (*Astounded*) Fair! Look, you moron, wake up! And don't touch that pair of electric points, the rheostat's not in yet. We'll use it on her if we need to in a minute. (*Throws third dart*)

QUARK   (*She has begun to sit on upstage centre seat on which the two leads for the imposition of electric shocks have been placed. As the base of her spine touches them she is thrown forward downstage*) AAAAAAAAAH!

SQUALOID   Oh bugger it. Is she alive?

QUARK   I've got multiple vision, like a fly's eyes!

KURU   (*Having run to her, placing her yellow gown round* QUARK's *shoulders*) She's blinded!

SQUALOID   You ruin everything, you mad fools. More damage is done by you women than by all the troops put together.

KURU   (*Arm round* QUARK) Before you do anything else to her, *I* told her the code in the garden. But she's only a child, she didn't realize what I was telling her, and I only said it in passing by mistake.

SQUALOID   Do you know what's at stake? (*Menacing*) What's coming?

KURU   Don't touch me, don't touch me! Don't come near her!

SQUALOID   Are you schizoid? She's not part of your own body. Look, even if she were, you can always breed another. If we ferret you.

KURU   Give my baby *some* dignity! Keep away!

SQUALOID   No one can hear you, see?

KURU   Keep away from me!

SQUALOID   There's no such thing as rape. (*With one wrench rips off* KURU's *bathing costume*)

KURU   (*With hatred*) The lie of the land! (*Warningly*) I'll bite its head off! Spit vinegar! I warn you! (SQUALOID *advances*) You're a killer!

KURU *seizes one electrode in each hand and shudders to death.*

QUARK   (*Blind; still downstage, on floor facing audience*) God is best seen when all the sky is dark. (*Pause*) What are you doing to her?

SQUALOID   Never you mind. (*He drags* KURU's *naked body upstage right to leave it there until he hangs it up at end of play*) Phagocyte!

Enter PHAGOCYTE *from stage right in shirtsleeves, dressed like* SQUALOID.

PHAGOCYTE   Here!

SQUALOID   She's croaked it. Things have gone wrong. Are you ready?

PHAGOCYTE   Jesus!

SQUALOID   Well, come on, man! The walls have shadows that whisper.

PHAGOCYTE   I can take it.

SQUALOID   You're damn lucky you're not detailed to combat the Shifta. In North-West Kenya. They cut your balls off and wear them in their buttonholes. I saw them skin a Spaniard called Raymon Cajal alive. Really; I mean it. They took his skin off in strips with razorblades. He looked like meat, screaming. (*Pause*) Right; bring him in. (*As* PHAGOCYTE *exits stage right to collect* CHALONE, SQUALOID *says, almost to himself*) He's going to talk.

SCENE NINE

Enter PHAGOCYTE *with* CHALONE. CHALONE *wears his officer's uniform, minus hat, but the tunic is undone.* PHAGOCYTE *pushes him roughly to* SQUALOID.

SQUALOID   Well, now. Shall we unlock the treasures of your mind?

CHALONE   I'll tell you (*Grimly*) all I know.

SQUALOID   (*Cheerfully*) You will. You've been well-briefed in anti-interrogation techniques. But let's forget the false stories; you can cut that out. We're friends here. (*To* PHAGOCYTE) Put him in the brain.

PHAGOCYTE *forces* CHALONE *to sit on interrogation seat, which is an upstage centre part of the brain.*

CHALONE   A doctor should be present.

SQUALOID   Phagocyte? You're a doctor.

PHAGOCYTE   Rightio.

CHALONE   No! Not the electrics!

SQUALOID   Only on your balls.

CHALONE   No!

SQUALOID   (*To audience, as* PHAGOCYTE *fastens* CHALONE *so that he is unable to escape*)

The junction between one nerve and the next is a synapse: the gap across which a chemical message passes. It can be measured electronically. That measurement is most easily appreciated when we give it a popular name such as 'pain'. (*Pause*) Is he fixed?

PHAGOCYTE   We're ready.

SQUALOID   Now, will you tell us what the news is? Oh, I know you've been taught how to detach yourself from pain; but Phagocyte here's never watched, and he wants to learn!

PHAGOCYTE   I hope it's never useful.

SQUALOID   You'll never be interrogated.

PHAGOCYTE   God forbid! Let's get on with it.

SQUALOID   But he doesn't want the electrics. We must be fair! Anyway, you can't decipher a telephone call by knowing the voltage. (PHAGOCYTE *produces a red-hot branding-iron*) What have you got there? A brand?

Now this really is power. (*Holding it, and moving it closer and closer to* CHALONE'*s face*) To say whether or not the iron touches him. (CHALONE *screams*) I haven't touched you yet. (*Pause*) Too crude. He could survive this. (*Hands back branding-iron*)

PHAGOCYTE   (*Takes branding-iron from* SQUALOID *and disposes of it*) I remember in Cairo, the enemy had got hold of some of our Gurkhas and shaved all the hair off their bodies. A terrible insult! Then let them go. Our boys went out and caught four of the enemy and brought them in, and the Warrant Officer said 'Out with their John Thomases.' Chop, chop, chop, chop. He had them off just like that! Then we sent them back in return. I know, I was there.

SQUALOID   Did it make them talk?

PHAGOCYTE   They weren't in much of a mood for a gossip. But we made another one talk. Taped his thumbs behind his back, then two tapes over his John Thomas, one that way, one this way. Then sat back and read a book, played chess. In eight hours he was writhing on the floor. He'll want to pee after four. Twelve to fourteen is the longest a man can go. One of the most painful things on earth. No sign left afterwards.

SQUALOID   You're no professional soldier; that's kids' play. Come on, we'll use the claw.

CHALONE   (*Violently*) NO!

PHAGOCYTE   The claw?

SQUALOID   Common or garden domestic soldering-iron. Insert it in his anus. (*To audience as well as to* PHAGOCYTE) It's good (*Picking it up and showing it*) because it's very cheap to work. Can be smuggled anywhere in a loaf of bread, and they stock them in Woolworths.

CHALONE   What can you want to know that I can't tell you without it?

SQUALOID   Right. Out you come.

               They bend CHALONE *over.*

SQUALOID   Better than having your skin peeled off, innit? (*To* PHAGOCYTE) Conscript, hold his head, will you?

PHAGOCYTE   I'm a volunteer.

SQUALOID   (*Violently*) You're a fucking conscript! (*Back to normal*) Give me your knife.

CHALONE   You shouldn't do this! We have only one body.

SQUALOID   (*Genially*) Just enlarging the opening for you. (*To audience*) The body will shudder at the sharp and unexpected prick of the knife.

SQUALOID *cuts.* CHALONE *screams, his whole body arches, and then falls flat on the floor.*

SQUALOID   Neat. Now, the seat. (*They drag him up and back to the seat, where* SQUALOID *pretends to insert from upstage side of* CHALONE, *i.e. behind him and thus out of sight of audience, the 'claw'. Gasp from* CHALONE *as it is assumed to go in*)

Would you plug the lead in the running flex? (*Pause*) *I'll* turn the switch on in a minute.

PHAGOCYTE   (*Quickly, bordering on panic*) After Cairo I'm still terrified by the sound of running water in a dark room.

SQUALOID   We could inject Scotophobin and induce a fear of the dark. But the claw is simple. In any given system the most complex is also the most miniaturized. You can do more with less.

CHALONE   (*Begins to vomit*)

SQUALOID   (*Registering distaste for* CHALONE's *bad manners*) This is going to take some time. (*To* CHALONE) Are you sitting comfortably? (*To* PHAGOCYTE) I'll switch it on, and in half an hour he'll talk. Meanwhile, you and I have lots to discuss.

PHAGOCYTE   (*Indicating* QUARK) What about her?

SQUALOID   She's blind. You can stare at her mastoids without her bothering. (*Rips off the top half of her bikini, exposing her breasts. She crawls to downstage left*)

SQUALOID *and* PHAGOCYTE *begin to play cards.*

SQUALOID   Bridge? Two dummy hands? Oh, for Christ's sake! The dummy has gone to bed with the Queen of Spades. A Jack in his hand and the Queen bare.

PHAGOCYTE   (*Stops playing*) I can't.

SQUALOID   In any two person zero sum game the outcome depends on probability. Dividing by zero's not the same thing as dividing by one. It remains the same. Depends on how the top's behaving, like a loose bikini. Very attractive.

PHAGOCYTE   Eh?

SQUALOID   That's why we're stuck till he talks. (*Explaining the cards*) If you divide a non-zero number by zero you get infinity. If you multiply a non-zero number by zero you get zero. It all depends on which way he jumps. And whether we believe him.

CHALONE   (*Quietly, as though nearly demented*) You wizards that peep and mutter!

SQUALOID   (*To* CHALONE) You know me better than to think you'll get out of it. (*To* PHAGOCYTE) That which is one is one, as the Chinese say. That which is not one is also one.

CHALONE   (*Mind clear*) I'm not a character in a play, I'm a human being! And like any human being I *am* contradictory, and forget what I've said.

SQUALOID   Now it's a sign of an inexperienced and untutored mind to think that your ideas are perfectly right and your opponent's perfectly wrong.

PHAGOCYTE   Basis of chess.

SQUALOID   You mean the opposite. (*To* CHALONE) Just think of yourself as the suffering servant. (*To* PHAGOCYTE) I'll tell you what. Work this out to kill time. There are three prisoners in a condemned cell, and they are told that two of them are to be shot in the morning. One of the three is our friend, and he has a chance of escape that he knows is nearly certain to fail. If he fails and is caught he'll certainly be shot. He has this evening, then, a one-in-three chance of living. Two of the three are to be shot, but they don't know which ones. Therefore one of the other two must obviously be shot, whether or not our friend is.

Now, why is it that, when the warder comes in and tells our friend in his ear the name of one of the other two who is to be shot, it increases our friend's hope of living? Prevents him trying to escape? His chances of survival are now not one in three but one in two. Evens. (*Pause*) Yet he knew one of the other two was to be shot, anyway. Why does the knowledge of a man's name change the odds?

PHAGOCYTE   I'm lost.

SQUALOID   Just riddles for life. Law's contradictions. Like the law of the excluded middle. Another bikini. X cannot be A and non-A, or neither A nor non-A. Good God! I forgot to turn the iron on.

PHAGOCYTE   I thought he was quiet.

SQUALOID   (*Turning on switch at junction of running flex and plugged lead from 'claw'*) Just think of youth in Asia.

CHALONE   (*Praying*) Keep me as the apple of an eye, under the shadow of thy wing.

SQUALOID   (*Taking* PHAGOCYTE *by shoulder and bringing him downstage right to sit at edge of stage.* QUARK *is in the same position stage left, but the light is off her and concentrated on* SQUALOID *and* PHAGOCYTE)

In order to study the nature of man you must study nature. (*Gestures to* PHAGOCYTE *to sit. Sits with him at his side*)

PHAGOCYTE   Nature? We saw a lot of foxes. They'd go on a killing spree, but the fox would always come back later to collect more of his kill. We'd go out when the wind was right and spread a ring of traps, six or eight gins – they're illegal now – round where he'd been killing. He usually came back the next night, unless he sniffed us; and once one leg was caught, his pawing the ground all round to get free would sometimes catch all four legs and the muzzle.

SQUALOID   We used to boil pigeons.

PHAGOCYTE   Ah, pigeons! Now there's a bird. I knew them better than anything. They eat three times a day, and when there's snow on the ground or a hard frost they'll pick the heart out of the middle of a Brussel sprout – you know, where it's nice and whitish when you've pulled the outer leaves off. When you get a flock of them on a nice field of Brussel sprouts you can imagine the damage they do. Like hares on sugar-beet. Those are terrors! When the sugar-beet is two leaves through the ground, they'll go and crop it. That's why we go on hare shoots in February.

SQUALOID   But the pigeons?

PHAGOCYTE   I can watch them for hours. Swing with all their weight on a pod of peas to bring it off the stalk on to the ground. Then, when it's fallen, peck it open. I cut a pigeon open once and found one hundred and twenty peas in its crop. That's counting every pea, the small ones as well. Now, if there's a thousand pigeons, you can see, they do no end of damage. (*Pause*) They sometimes go over a crop of clover and do it good. They bite the heads off the young plants, and two or three will grow in their place. Same as when the wheat crop is gathering well. From one kernel of corn, five or six on the stalk, if your land's in good condition. I love the smell of freshly split peas in pod.

SQUALOID   (*Surprised*) The suborned wing! Oh, nothing. I suppose your pea and your cherry are only inferior olives; just as the common pigeon's only a dirty dove, if you think about it. We shouldn't grouse. Now grouse is an overrated bird. It ranks too high.

PHAGOCYTE   Not when you get used to it. Oh, I used to know those fens almost as a person: in all lights and seasons. I understood them.

SQUALOID   They say every farmer farms for his son.

PHAGOCYTE   Travellers' Joy becomes Old Man's Beard in September. With wheat, if you don't do something about burning the flag off you'll get mildew, and then if there's a storm it will knock it flat. The devil to harvest. You can spray against it, though; with helicopters. Diluted acid from the air.

SQUALOID   Amazing what you can do with defoliants.

PHAGOCYTE   Pigeons don't build till June or July. We push them out of their nests with poles; in the hedges, to smash their eggs. Oh, yes. If you get a nice Indian summer, you'll get pigeons nesting again for the second time. I saw some a month ago.

SQUALOID   Did you fish in the fens?

PHAGOCYTE   Often. Eels. But you've got to watch it. When you cut the head off an eel you have to be very careful taking the hook out of its mouth. Even when the head's off the body some time, he can still bite your finger off. Don't ask me how. I love eels. My Mum and Dad did, too. Jellied. A muggy night, thundery, is best. They don't like a full moon in the sky. Any fisherman will tell you, a heavy, dark night's the best for eels. We get big ones; five and six pounds. Now abroad, congers go up to a hundred pounds. Serpents! Thick as you are.

SQUALOID   Eh?

PHAGOCYTE   Round the waist. Get eels in a fossil pit and they grow pretty big in England, too. I've one in a drain-pipe in a pond in my garden. Feed him lob worms. All those worms, lying about on the lawn when the sun's down. They may have no eyes, those worms, but they've sensitive skin. If I search the grass for them with too bright a torch they'll shoot back down their holes at once. But my eel knows my torch. Not like wild eels. When he sees my torch he knows he's going to be fed. People say you needn't be quiet when eel-fishing, but they're wrong. Mine in his pipe can hear my footfall on the crazy-paving. Now a conger eel will pull you out of the boat. He'll drag you down to the bottom until you drown. They always swim along the bottom. Once in the boat, he'll thrash around until the line's all caught up in your legs, then plop! over the side and in you go after it. My mate drowned that way. Depressed me. Put me off eels for a while, that did.

SQUALOID   Did they give you electric shocks?

PHAGOCYTE   No, it's the electric eel that gives you the shock. Enough to stun a man. I put two smaller ordinary eels in my pond as a bit of companionship for mine, and you should have seen the water thrash! The big eel biting the others by the tail and churning the water with them till they both climbed out on to the lawn. I threw them back, and finally he killed them. I love eels. (*Pause*) I went to the London zoo, and saw two in a tank, and I just don't understand why they don't fight. In rivers they can swim away; but in my pond . . . Well, that's his territory. Still, they're half asleep in winter.

CHALONE *leaps up from seat and staggers.* SQUALOID *seizes gun and holds it at hip, pointing, moving to stage left.* PHAGOCYTE *is stage right, standing now, and* CHALONE *centrestage.*

SQUALOID   Get him! Right! You want to live, do you? Life is worth living. But only just. So, to give him the benefit of the doubt . . .

SQUALOID *shoots* PHAGOCYTE.

CHALONE   (*Walking over to* SQUALOID) Well done. Did you have to shoot him dead though?

SQUALOID   Yes. I promised him I would. (*They shake hands*)

CHALONE   Eh? (*Looking at dead body of* PHAGOCYTE) We depend on others for ourselves. That's why the final moments are so terrifying.

SQUALOID   You acted well.

CHALONE   He gave away the information.

SQUALOID   More than he thought. It was also clear he'd had my girl.

CHALONE   That's why you shot him!

SQUALOID   He would have squealed, anyway. The closing phase of a war is no time to be taken prisoner by the losing side. They'll be here by tonight, even if we do eventually win the war. If he'd been caught, he would have betrayed us.

CHALONE   And you?

SQUALOID   If taken, I will accept the law of the vanquished.

CHALONE   (*Looking at* PHAGOCYTE) The deed is executed. Only the strong can afford weakness.

SQUALOID   Look at his neck. Stretched out stiff like a swan in flight.

CHALONE   Pretending is extraordinarily exhausting. It's terribly hard work. (*Looking at* PHAGOCYTE's *face*) Sympathy is innocence.

SQUALOID   No. Sympathy is impotence. Withdrawal of sympathy is essential if one is to get anything done, let alone interrogation.

CHALONE   (*Wryly*) There's no such thing as 'torture', I suppose?

SQUALOID   We believe in abstract justice for everybody. That doesn't involve us with anyone. If you look at any person objectively, it induces a measure of contempt.

CHALONE   Who for?

SQUALOID   (*Sharply*) Come off it, who do you think? You are at a disadvantage, being cursed with a strong imagination. When you meet a girl, you think through to the post-coital disgust and exhaustion, and so don't even begin.

CHALONE That's what love is: the shutter that comes down to prevent you thinking. (*Doing up tunic*) Well, if you're going to do a morning's work, you might as well wear a morning coat.

SQUALOID I suppose you'll want to see him when he's ready?

CHALONE Yes.

SQUALOID I'll have him brought up to the chapel of rest so you can say good-bye. (*Laying out* PHAGOCYTE *onstage where he is lying*) When I'd seen my Mother, she looked so at peace. She had all her teeth, and looked as though I'd wake her at once if I touched her. I only went because I knew my Father would like me to. But when *he* had gone, I had no particular reason to see him. Yet there is a sort of completeness, especially if it's your own parent and you weren't there during the final moments. It does round things off. Anyway, the undertaker who'd laid out my Mother assumed I would want the same with my Father, so I went in. This time the napkin was still over his face, so I stepped over and took it off. His jaw had dropped open and locked, his tongue had curled back in his mouth, and without his false teeth his face looked totally different, quite apart from the colour. I suddenly hated him. Yet two days before he had been sitting up, repeating himself endlessly as he tried to concentrate on what day my sister was coming to visit him, and I'd felt nothing but tenderness. I'm not unfeeling.

CHALONE It takes three generations to bury a man.

SQUALOID Oh, they soon forget your resting-place.

CHALONE Every time I kill, it brings back the smell of mist and woodsmoke, those sudden dusks in India: the cow-dust hour, when everything hangs in the air—jasmine, temple flowers . . .

SQUALOID Don't think. It's only the price of time.

CHALONE Peace is the breathing space between two wars; when we lick our wounds, mourn our dead, and prepare our defences.

SQUALOID   When we reached Belsen at the end of the last, I soon learned not to waste time with the old or any with typhoid. Only the young, only those we had a chance of saving. We'd had no medical training, but we all had to help. When I tried to use a needle intravenously, the poor devils wouldn't let me and yelled out 'Nicht Krematorium! Nicht Krematorium!' The Deutsch had been injecting them with paraffin so they'd burn better. (*Pause*) The Nazis have come and gone.

CHALONE   And the memory remains.

QUARK   I am full of love for my teddy-bear. And my Mummy and Daddy, and my grandparents. God bless everyone!

CHALONE   (*Startled, going over to look at her*) A feather dropped from the plumage of heaven!

SQUALOID   (*Dragging body of* PHAGOCYTE *across stage from down right to upstage left*) That was an error. We all make these inaccuracies at times. If we survive, there's plenty of time to repent.

CHALONE   (*Looking at* QUARK) Let your love lighten upon the waste of our wraths and sorrows.

SQUALOID   Are you praying? I haven't tidied him up yet!

CHALONE   Yes, one prays, of course. But the thought always returns; he saved others, himself he cannot save.

SQUALOID   Leave her. Give me a hand.

CHALONE *goes upstage left to take over from* SQUALOID, *and hang* PHAGOCYTE *from hook, while* SQUALOID *goes over to stage right and hoists up naked body of* KURU. PHAGOCYTE *and* KURU *may stand on black boxes against a black background. The impression must be given of two bodies hanging from wrists, male clothed, female unclothed, at the same position upstage right and left, faces upstage.*

The work complete, CHALONE *and* SQUALOID *come downstage centre at the same time.*

SQUALOID   Have you ever heard the sound of birds in Trafalgar Square late at night, when it's floodlit and there's not a soul around? Unnatural. (*Pause*) I've always imagined that as the only sound left at the end of the world.

CHALONE   Birds are divine remembrancers.

SQUALOID   What shall we do with his suitcase?

CHALONE   Use his clothes to mop up his blood, then burn the lot.

Cockcrow offstage.

SQUALOID   That's odd. (*Lights begin to fade*) We don't usually hear cockerels in towns. I was right out in the middle of no-man's land, and dark had just begun to hint the feeling of dawn, when far in the distance, right on the edge of silence, there was the crow of a cock. Then a long moment later, almost as far away, another answered. Nothing but that. (*Pause*) Then right beside me! Coarse, raucous, jumping me out of my skin.

CHALONE   The musical equivalent of first light.

SQUALOID   You don't hear that in towns.

CHALONE   Man made.

SQUALOID   Man devised.

CHALONE   Mandarin man destroys.

SQUALOID   Oh, fear is the womb of war, which a little violence will awake. We'll repair the waste cities.

CHALONE   Money's a shadow. (*To audience*) The parts of actors are like the flames of matches, blown out in the wind, and vanished. Pray for those whose mouths last week were stopped by human violence, with dust.

Snap blackout after brief pause.

END

A Play to Remember

Harold Hobson's review of Killing Time.
(THE SUNDAY TIMES, 7.ix.75)

(Having reviewed Athol Fugard's *Dimetos*, which received high praise, and two other plays which received less.)

More theatrically significant is Francis Warner's *Killing Time* (Jordanburn). The thesis of this surrealistically imaginative play is that what distinguishes man from every other living thing is his tendency to suicide. Even lemmings struggle to get to the other shore. But both in explicit speech and in a startling Dadaistic scene in which a nude girl (Andee Cromarty) escapes from the guillotine to dance a beautifully delicate lyrical poem, the play suggests the possibility that that part of the brain which leads to suicide may also one day bring us to fuller life. Yet this I suspect is with Mr Warner but a fleeting hope. Like Fugard's *Dimetos*, *Killing Time* with scenes of war and woe and whores, is not for all markets, but where it is appreciated it will fetch a high price.

Fringe Benefits

Harold Hobson's review of the London Production of Meeting Ends.
(THE SUNDAY TIMES, 28.iv.74)

Till now the Fringe theatres have lacked intrepidity. But new life is coming to them. Francis Warner, in *Meeting Ends* (New End), without flinching tells a permissive age the unpalatable truth that, though there is pleasure in sex, this pleasure does not last. Moreover the play is experimental, which Fringe theatres almost invariably fail to be. Their notions of avant-garde productions are founded on Brecht, Pirandello and Artaud, all of whom have been dead just long enough for them to be quaint and old-fashioned. Even when they incorporate the great name of Grotowski, they are essentially derivative. That is why the production of Mr Warner's play is an exciting event.

Most people will see that in 'Meeting Ends' there is a lot of nudity. What is not so immediately apparent is that Mr Warner uses this nudity partly for erotic and startling effects, but principally as a means of creative expression. I have never seen this done before. Mr Warner's echoing prose and his stately verse are sometimes baffling. He makes references that are not in every child's lexicon. There is even a scene, remarkably played by Josephine McNamara, in which a naked young woman caresses herself in a high wind, after taking a bath and deciding not to urinate, that might cause the stuffy-minded to fall into a coma of misgiving. But whatever may be one's reaction to these things, it would be foolish to deny that, in 'Meeting Ends', Fringe theatre has uniquely produced something that is absorbingly experimental, forward-looking and brave, as well as, at times, in no equivocal sense, beautiful.

The theme is Mithraic. Ensoff, a noble figure (Charles West), in Oxford Chancellor's robes, has imaginatively created a world in which chastity is constantly assaulted by the aggressiveness of sex. Three women are held in pillories. One of them (Katharine Schofield) is wearing a bathing dress, which a man, Shango (Simon Cuff) rips off her, leaving her naked. But before the clothed figure of another woman, Agappy (Evie Garratt), he kneels in homage, nude except for his bull's head. Thereafter nakedness is used invariably as representative of weakness, surrender, submission, and the moments when it appears, and when the bull's head is finally rejected, have high significance. They culminate in the sensational castration of Ensoff by Shango, an incident that is less a victory for the aggressor than for the victim, who presumably may be taken as expressing Mr Warner's own judgment when he says

> *The silent stars play havoc with our toys,*
> *But we have kingdoms that they cannot touch.*

All the players gave poised and eloquent performances.